Generis

PUBLISHING

Judiciary in Bangladesh

Md. Milan Hossain

Title: **Judiciary in Bangladesh**

ISBN: 979-8-89248-764-1

Author: Md. Milan Hossain

Cover image: www.pixabay.com

Publisher: Generis Publishing
Online orders: www.generis-publishing.com
Contact email: info@generis-publishing.com

Judiciary in Bangladesh

Md. Milan Hossain

Dedicated to My Parents, my PhD Mentor and my Family

Acknowledgement

Judiciary is an important organ of the government which can ensure justice only if it works independently, separately i.e. without any interference other organs of the government, fairly by competent judges. In conducting this book, I depend on my PhD thesis titled 'Judiciary and Citizens Rights: Bangladesh Perspective (Not-Published) and the journal papers published in home and abroad.

I am very grateful to my honorable PhD supervisor, Prof. Dr. Abdul Latif Masum for his guidance, advice, encouragement and support at all levels. I would like to express my special thanks to Adv. Hiramoti Khanam, Adv. Mousowmi Akter, Adv. Mahmudul Islam, my students Shaparwan, Sumon, Akhter for their valuable assistance in collecting data for the research.

I would like to thank my family and friends for their wonderful support and continuous encouragement. My highest appreciation is reserved for my beloved wife – Mrs. Nusrat Jahan, Additional District Judge, BJCS, for her continuous support, encouragement, and assistance on my research work.

Without supervision, advice, suggestion, comments, assistance of the mentioned scholars, academicians, non-academicians, my colleagues, friends, students and my family members I could not have completed this work.

Abstract

The book contains seven chapters focusing upon outlines of judiciary in Bangladesh, Subordinate Judiciary and Citizens' Rights in Bangladesh, Higher Judiciary and Citizens' Rights in Bangladesh, The Separation of Judiciary in Bangladesh-Constitutional Mandates and *Masdar Hossain Case's* Directions, Judiciary and Rule of Law in the Post Separation Period –An Evaluation, Judiciary and Citizens' Right to Life, Liberty and Right against Inhuman Treatment or Punishment in Bangladesh, Backlog of Cases-Civil & Criminal Justice in Bangladesh. In doing so, the author depends on his PhD thesis titled Judiciary and Citizens Rights: Bangladesh Perspective and different published papers.

Key Words: Judiciary, Citizens Rights, Separation of Judiciary, Rule of Law, Backlog of Cases

ACRONYMS

ADR	: Alternative Dispute Resolution
AD	: Appellate Division
ADR	: Alternative Dispute Resolution
BLD	: Bangladesh Legal Digest
CD	: Case Diary
CrPC	: Code of Criminal Procedure
CPC	: Civil Code Procedure
CJM	: Chief Judicial Magistrate
CR	: Complaint Register
DLR	: Dhaka Law Reports
FIR	: First Information Report
GR	: General Register
HCD	: High Court Division
PS	: Police Station
SC	: Supreme Court
SD	: Settling Date
SCOB	: Supreme Court Online Bulletin

CONTENTS

Chapter-One:

The Outlines of Judiciary in Bangladesh[1]

Introduction

Judiciary is an important organ of a State, the responsibility of which is to ensure, protect, enforce people rights either constitutional or statutory and overall the responsibility is to establish the rule of law and examine the activities of the executive, legislature and even the activities of itself. It is rightly said that "the judiciary stands between the people of the country and the State as a bulwark against Executive pressure, excesses and misuse of power by the Executive" (61 DLR 523, Para- 208).

Generally, the judiciary of a country comprises all courts and tribunals which interpret law, settle legal disputes, enforce rights of citizens and impose penalty to the offenders. What are overall outlines of current judiciary of Bangladesh? What is the evaluation of current judiciary? Whether this judiciary can ensure justice due time? What are existing basic problems of current judiciary? all these are matters of research. Under considering all these matters, this chapter has been drawn.

1.1. Historical Background

After independence of Bangladesh, the High Court of East Pakistan was turned into the name of High Court of Bangladesh by the High Court of Bangladesh Order, 1972 which was adapted on 17th January 1972.[2]

The High Court consisted of Chief Justice and other judges who were appointed by the president. The term and conditions also were determined by the president. The High Court of Bangladesh as a Court of Record[3] had original, appellate, revisional, review, special, procedure and all other powers as exercised by the

---

[1] Author depends in conducting the chapter upon his PhD thesis titled 'Judiciary and Citizens Rights: Bangladesh Perspective (Not-Published) and the journal paper published in the title of 'Outlines of Current Judiciary of Bangladesh: A Study' 4,Asia-Pacific Law & Policy Review,2018

[2] Hoque, Kazi Ebadul, *Administration of Justice in Bangladesh,* 1st Edition, Asiatic Society of Bangladesh, Dhaka, 2003, p. 26.

[3] See, Article 108 of *the Constitution of the Peoples' Republic of Bangladesh, 1972*

High Court of East Pakistan but it could not exercise any issue of writ.[4] This power was banned by the High Court of Bangladesh (Amendment) Order 1972 (President Order No. 91 of 1972)[5] After passing the Act, it established an Appellate Division of the High Court of Bangladesh consisting of one chief justice and other judges appointed by the president with the consultation of chief justice.[6] The purpose of establishing appellate Division was to deal with all appeals and petitions, pending before Supreme Court of Pakistan, arisen in East Pakistan. The President Order No. 91 of 1972 also provided to follow the rules made by erstwhile Supreme Court of Pakistan.[7] All functions of the subordinate court and magistracy court were unchanged and continued under the laws of Continuance Enforcement Order 1971. [8] All judges and officers of the subordinate court acted under the supervision of High Court of Bangladesh.

1.2. Current Judicial System in Bangladesh

The current Judiciary of Bangladesh can be drawn broadly by the Supreme Court (higher judiciary) and subordinate courts (lower judiciary). The highest court in Bangladesh is known as the Supreme Court of Bangladesh having two divisions- a) the High Court Division and b) the Appellate Division (Bangladesh Constitution, Art. 94) (hereinafter as the Constitution). Subordinate courts may be civil, criminal, special or tribunal.

1.2.1. Supreme Court of Bangladesh

Now, **Supreme Court** is the highest court of Bangladesh. The Supreme Court comprises with Appellate Division and High Court Division. It consists of the Chief Justice and other judges.[9] According to Article 94(4) of the Constitution; it ensures the judges to exercise their judicial function independently. It means no body of government organization will interfere the function of judges. It is the last resort of the aggrieved person.

The Chief Justice and other judges are appointed by the president.[10] To be a judge, he must be a citizen of Bangladesh and he must have 10 years'

---

[4] Hoque, Kazi Ebadul, *Administration of Justice in Bangladesh,* 1st Edition, Asiatic Society of Bangladesh, Dhaka, 2003, p. 27.
[5] *Ibid*
[6] *The High Court of Bangladesh Order 1972,* Sec 3.
[7] Hoque, Kazi Ebadul, *Administration of Justice in Bangladesh,* 1st Edition, Asiatic Society of Bangladesh, Dhaka, 2003, p. 27.
[8] *Ibdi, p. 26*
[9] *The Constitution of the Peoples' Republic of Bangladesh 1972, Art 94 (2).*
[10] *Ibid, Art 95 (1).*

experience as advocate of Supreme Court or 10 years' experience as judicial officer in Bangladesh or qualified by law.[11] They shall hold the office till attaining sixty seven years old. Before 7th & 14th amendment of Constitution, the retirement age of judges was subsequently till 62 & 65 years old.[12] The president empowered to remove judge from office on the basis of the report of Supreme Judicial Council.[13] In case of vacancy of the office of Chief Justice, the vacancy shall be filled up by the next most senior judge of Appellate Division to perform the functions of Supreme Court.[14] President may also appoint Additional Supreme Court Judges. Supreme Court shall be situated at Dhaka as capital of Bangladesh. Supreme Court also is empowered to make rule and review the judgment of it.[15] Its decision is binding for all courts.[16]

The Higher Court in Bangladesh is independent from any interference of other organ of the government that is recognized by the Constitution of Bangladesh under Article 94 (4), 116A, 112, 109 and 22 as well as well-recognized case, ***Masdar Hossain, Anwar Hossain vs Bangladesh*** and 16th amendment case. According to Article 114, there shall be established sub-ordinate court of Supreme Court in Bangladesh which may be formed by law.[17] In a broad sense, subordinate court can be divided into two categories namely, Civil Court; Criminal Court. Supreme Court is divided in to appellate division and high court division.

1.2.1a The High Court Division

High Court Division has both original and appellate jurisdiction as well as the power to issue writ, order and direction in the nature of habeas corpus, mandamus, prohibition, quo warranto or certiorari.[18] It has power to control and superintendence over all court and subordinate to it.[19] The jurisdiction of the high court division may be divided in to two:

1. Ordinary or general jurisdiction
2. Constitutional jurisdiction

---

[11] *Ibid, Art 95 (2).*
[12] *Ibid, Art 96 (1).*
[13] *Ibid, Art 96 (6).*
[14] *Ibid, Art 97.*
[15] *Ibid, Art 105 & 107.*
[16] *Ibid, Art 111.*
[17] *The Constitution of the Peoples' Republic of Bangladesh 1972, Art 114.*
[18] *Ibid, Art 1972, Art 101 & 102 (2).*
[19] *Ibid, Art 109.*

1.2.1bThe Appellate Division

Appellate Division is empowered to hear appeals from judgments, Decrees, Orders or Sentences of the High Court Division.[20] Appeals as of right can be filed before Appellate Division on the ground of interpretation of statute, death sentence, life imprisonment, punishment for contempt of court.[21] It has also power to review the judgments or order by it.[22] Beside this it has advisory jurisdiction.[23] The appellate division of Supreme Court has no original jurisdiction but it has appellate Jurisdiction only the appellate court classifies below:

1. Ordinary or General Jurisdiction.
2. Constitutional jurisdiction.

1.2.2. Subordinate Courts

Subordinate courts may be known as lower judiciary of country referring to the courts as civil, criminal, special or tribunal etc. Upon considering the functions of courts the subordinate courts are of broadly civil and criminal. By the separation of judiciary from the executive in 2007, actually the magistrate courts are separated from the executive and from that time these magistrate courts are termed as judicial magistrate courts and for that some changes have been brought in the Code of Criminal Procedure, 1908 (hereinafter as CrPC).

1.2.2a Civil Courts

Civil courts are those courts which have jurisdiction to try all suits of a civil nature, i. e. a suit in which the right to property, post or an office is contested except its cognizance is expressly or impliedly barred by any law (CPC, Section 9). Therefore, when citizens' individual legal rights or private rights e.g. right to property, post or office are affected, citizens can seek the remedies from the civil courts. There are five classes of civil courts recognized by the Civil Courts (Amendment) Act, 2001(Act No. XLIX of 2001) in Bangladesh, namely:

- The Court of the District Judge
- The court of Additional District Judge

---

[20] *Ibid, Art 103.*
[21] *Ibid, Art 103 (2).*
[22] *Ibid, Art 105.*
[23] *Ibid, Art 106* [cited in Akkas, Sarkar Ali, *Independence and Accountability of Judiciary: A Critical Review*, 1st Edition, Centre for Rights and Governance, Dhaka, 2004, p. 89].

- ☞ The Court of Joint District Judge
- ☞ The Court of Senior Assistant Judge
- ☞ The Court of Assistant Judge

Among them, the District Court is subordinate to the High Court Division, and every Civil Court of a grade inferior to that of a District Court (CPC, Section 3). Besides, the Constitution declares that the High Court Division has superintendence and control over all courts and subordinate to it (Art.109).

The Court of District Judge:

District judge is the head of civil judiciary in each district.[24] It has administrative control over all civil courts situated in local limits.[25] They are appointed through promotion form the amongst additional district judge. A District Judge generally does not deal with original suits[26] but in certain cases it tries the cases related to insolvency, probate and administration, Trade Marks related issues etc. Its pecuniary jurisdiction is unlimited.[27] It is also empowered to transfer the cases and appeals to the Additional District Judge or any other civil court under its control.[28] It is empowered to control all civil courts next to HCD within its territory.[29] The court is authorized to transfer, withdraw any suit, appeal and other proceedings in any civil courts below HCD.[30] It is remarkable that the Court can exercise the revisional power under section 115 of the Code of Civil Procedure 1983, on the ground of error of law or failure of justice caused by the inferior court of it. In case of appeal and revision, the pecuniary jurisdiction is till five lacs.[31] In a case ***Bangladesh v A.H.M Khurshed Ali***, it is held that where the valuation of the subject matter of proceeding exceeds five lacs then the revisional application shall lie to the HCD under section 115(1) of CPC.[32] Besides these, District Judge is also acted as a Session Judge to adjudicate criminal cases.[33] Its jurisdiction is as follows:

1. Pecuniary jurisdiction
2. Appellate jurisdiction

---

[24] Halim, Md. Abdul, *The Legal System of Bangladesh,* 8th Edition, CCB Foundation, Dhaka, 2014, p. 110.
[25] *The Civil Court Act 1887, Sec 9.*
[26] Halim, Md. Abdul, *The Legal System of Bangladesh,* 8th Edition, CCB Foundation, Dhaka, 2014, p. 110.
[27] *Ibid.*
[28] *The Civil Court Act 1887,* Sec 08, 11, 22, 23.
[29] *Ibid*
[30] *The Civil Court Act 1887, Sec 24.*
[31] Hoque, Kazi Ebadul, *Administration of Justice in Bangladesh,* 1st Edition, Asiatic Society of Bangladesh, Dhaka, 2003, p. 36.
[32] 14 MLR (AD) 57
[33] Halim, Md. Abdul, *The Legal System of Bangladesh,* 8th Edition, CCB Foundation, Dhaka, 2014, p. 111.

3. Administration and transfer jurisdiction.
4. Revisional jurisdiction
5. Double capacity

Courts of Additional District Judge:

The court of additional district is comprised with the additional district judge who is appointed through promotion amongst the joint distinct judge. His pecuniary jurisdiction is unlimited. Usually he tries those cases which are transfer to his court from the court of the district judge.[34] Sometimes he is appointed as additional session judge. Appeal against the decision of this court lies to the High Court Division.[35]

The Court of the Joint District Judge:

They are appointed through the promotion from amongst the senior assistant judges. The court has original and appellate jurisdictions. Its pecuniary jurisdiction states with taka 25 lack plus to unlimited.[36] Sometimes it acts as a small cases court and Joint Session Judge.[37] The court hears the appeals imposed upon it by the District Judge against the order or decree of a Senior Assistant Judge or Assistant Judge.[38] Appeals against Senior Assistant Judge or Assistant Judge may be transferred to the Joint District Judge by the District Judge.[39]

The Courts of Senior Assistant Judge:

This court is consisted with a senior assistant judge. They are appointed through promotion of amongst assistant judge. It's a pecuniary jurisdiction does not exceed 25 lacs taka but not less than 15 lacs. Appeal against this court lies to the District Judge Court. It acts as Small Causes Court.[40] Besides this, it also acts as Family Court and Election Tribunal consecutively under the Family Courts Ordinance, 1985 and Local Government (Upzilla Parishad) Ordinance, 1983.[41]

---

[34] *Ibid*
[35] *The Civil Court Act 1887*, Sec 20.
[36] Halim, Md. Abdul, *The Legal System of Bangladesh,* 8th Edition, CCB Foundation, Dhaka, 2014, p. 112.
[37] *The Civil Court Act 1887*, Sec 25.
[38] S *The Civil Court Act 1887*, Sec 22.
[39] Halim, Md. Abdul, *The Legal System of Bangladesh,* 8th Edition, CCB Foundation, Dhaka, 2014, p. 113.
[40] *The Civil Court Act 1887*, Sec 25.
[41] Halim, Md. Abdul, *The Legal System of Bangladesh,* 8th Edition, CCB Foundation, Dhaka, 2014, p. 113.

The Court of Assistant Judge:

This court shall be consisted with an assistant judge. Its pecuniary jurisdiction does not exceed 2 lack taka. It has small revisional power in all petty civil cases coming from village courts under the Village Courts Ordinance 1976.[42] It acts as Small Causes Court. Appeal from this court files before the Court of District Judge. There is no provision regarding second appeal in CPC. The provisions of second appeal under sections 100, 101 and 103 have been repelled by the Laws Reforms Ordinance, 1978[43]

1.2.2b Special Tribunal in Civil Nature

Special tribunal established in our legal system in two ways.

1. Established by constitution
2. Established by statute

Special Tribunal under Constitution

The formation and function of the administrative tribunal deals with the constitution. Article 117 of the Constitution of Bangladesh recognizes the Administrative tribunals. It stipulates parliament may by law establish one or more administrative tribunal to exercise jurisdiction of matters relating to, the terms and conditions, punishment of public servant, the acquisition, administration, management and disposal of property.[44] Where an administrative tribunal is existed, no court shall entertain any proceedings or matters fallen within the jurisdiction of tribunal.[45] There are two types of tribunal such as; Administrative Tribunal and Administrative Appellate Tribunal.[46]

Administrative Tribunal:

Administrative tribunal is not under the control of executive body or administrative department of the government.[47] It is a quasi-judicial body but not absolutely administrative in nature.[48] In ***Mujibur Rahman v. Bangladesh***

---

[42] See, Section 4(2) of *the Civil Court Act 1887* [cited in Halim, Md. Abdul, *The Legal System of Bangladesh,* 8th Edition, CCB Foundation, Dhaka, 2014, p. 113.

[43] Halim, Md. Abdul, *The Legal System of Bangladesh,* 8th Edition, CCB Foundation, Dhaka, 2014, p. 114.

[44] *The Constitution of the Peoples' Republic of Bangladesh 1972,* Art 117 (1).

[45] *Ibid, Art 117 (2).*

[46] Halim, Md. Abdul, *The Legal System of Bangladesh,* 8th Edition, CCB Foundation, Dhaka, 2014, p. 141.

[47] Takwani, C.K, *Lectures On Administrative Law,* 5th Edition, Eastern Book Company, Lucknow, 2012, p. 243.

[48] *Ibid.*

M.H. Rahman J also was drawn the same statement.[49] In a case namely ***Banglades v. A.K.M Zahingir*** held that any tribunal which is not invested with some part of the judicial power of the Republic is outside the ambit of art. 102 (5). To run Administrative tribunal parliament passed an Act namely "Administrative Tribunal Act 1980" and Administrative Tribunal Rules were also made in 1982.[50] Administrative tribunal deals such disputes which are relating to employment between the government and its employers. Each administrative Tribunal consists of one member who is appointed by the government from amongst person who is or has been district judge.[51] It has exclusive jurisdiction to have and determine application made by any persons in the service of the people republic of a statutory public authority in respect of the terms and conditions of his service against the decision of departmental authority.[52]

Administrative Appellate Tribunal

According to section 5 of the Administrative Tribunal Act, 1980 the Tribunal consists one chairman and two members. The Chairman is appointed from among the persons who are or have been judges of the Supreme Court and amongst two members one is a Joint Secretary and other is a District Judge. Section 6 provides the aggrieved person have to file appeal, against the decision of Administrative Tribunal, within three months from the date of order or decision. According to section 6 an appeal against the decision or order of Appellate Tribunal shall be filed before the Appellate Division of the Supreme Court due to leave to appeal as per article 103 of the Constitution of Bangladesh.[53]

Special Tribunal under Statute

Labour Court

The Government may by notification in the official gazette establish one or more labour court as it necessary.[54] A labour court shall be consisted of a chairman and two members but in respect of any matter under chapter ten and twelve it shall be consisted by of a chairman alone.[55] Among two members, one

---

[49] Islam, Mahmudul, *Constitutional law of Bangladesh*, 3rd Edition, Mullick Brothers, 2012, 578.
[50] Halim, Md. Abdul, *The Legal System of Bangladesh,* 8th Edition, CCB Foundation, Dhaka, 2014, p. 141.
[51] *The Administrative Tribunals Act 1980, Sec 3.*
[52] Halim, Md. Abdul, *The Legal System of Bangladesh,* 8th Edition, CCB Foundation, Dhaka, 2014, p. 142.
[53] *Ibid, p. 143.*
[54] *The Bangladesh Labour Code 2006, Sec 214.*
[55] *Ibid, Sec 214 (3).*

of the members is to represent the workmen and the other to represent the employers.[56]

The chairman may be appointed from the district judges or additional district judge.[57] The members shall be appointed after consultation with the employers and workmen. According to the Labour Act, 2006 a labour court shall have exclusive jurisdiction on the following matters namely[58]:

- To adjudicate and determine industries dispute on to try any offence under this Act.
- To examine and adjudicate any implementation on violations of a settlement which is referred by the government.
- To exercise any rower referred by this code.

The provisions contain in chapter 35 of the Code of Criminal Procedure (CrPC), 1898 shall apply to labour court.[59] According to the Section 215 of Labour Act, 2006, this court shall follow summary trial procedure as stated under CrPC to try any offence. It has the same power as like the first class magistrate under the CrPC to try any offence and for the purpose of punishment it has the same power as like court of session.[60] According to section 216 of the Labour Act, 2006 except the adjudicating and determining any criminal cases this court shall be deemed as a civil court. In a case ***Pubali Bank vs. the Chairman, 1st Labour Court***[61] it is held that Labour court acts as Civil Court for limited purpose but not a Civil Court at all.[62] The court shall prohibit strike or lock-out.[63] Any party aggrieved against the order or decision of the tribunal may lie an appeal to the Labour Appellate Tribunal.[64]

Labour Appellate Tribunal

According to the sec 218 of Labour Act, 2006, labour appellate tribunal shall be consisted by chairman and such number of members and such chairman shall be appointed from among person who is one has been a judge or an additional judge of the Supreme Court or is or has been a District Judge for at least three

[56] *Ibid, Sec 214 (6).*
[57] *Ibid, Sec 214 (4).*
[58] *Ibid, Sec 214 (10).*
[59] *Ibid, Sec 214 (12).*
[60] *Ibid, Sec 215 (2, 3).*
[61] *44 DLR (AD) 40.*
[62] Halim, Md. Abdul, *Textbook on Bangladesh Labour Code,* 8th Edition, CCB Foundation, Dhaka, 2017, p. 284.
[63] *The Bangladesh Labour Code 2006, Sec 225.*
[64] Hoque, Kazi Ebadul, *Administration of Justice in Bangladesh,* 1st Edition, Asiatic Society of Bangladesh, Dhaka, 2003, p.47.

year. Labour tribunal shall follow as namely as possible the provision of Civil Code Procedure to hear appeal.[65] This tribunal has power to modification awarded decision, judgment or section given by the labour court. If any person aggrieved on the decision of the labour appellate tribunal than the aggrieved person may appeal to the High Court Division.[66] The judgment of the tribunal shall be delivered within sixty days from the date of filling appeal.[67] It may pronounce a punishment for any term, or to pay fine exceeding two thousand taka.[68] Appeal against the court may file/prefer to the High Court Division.[69]

The Artha Rin-Adalat

The Artha Rin Adalat was established under section 104 of the Artha-Rin-Adalat Ain 2003. Every financial institution as listed in section 2 will file suits for recovery of money against a loan under this Act. This Adalat follows its own proceeding as well as the proceeding of CPC and application will be filed to the court through affidavits. A joint district judge will be appointed as judge of this court.

Land Survey Tribunal:

Land survey tribunal has been established under chapter (xvii) section 145 (A) of the State Acquisition and Tenancy Act (1950). This chapter has been added in 2004 by an amendment in the Act. As many Land Survey Tribunal as necessary to deal the suits related to record of rights made under section 144 of the Act. Government may determine and alter the territorial limits of jurisdiction regarding any Land Survey Tribunal.[70] In appointing judges of the tribunal, the government with the consultation of the Supreme Court appoints judges of the Land Survey Tribunal amongst the Joint District Judges.[71]

Land Survey Appellate Tribunal

Government may by the notification of the official Gazette set up Land Survey Appellate Tribunal to hear appeals which is filled against the order or decision of Land Survey Tribunal.[72] Government may also fix and alter the territorial

---

65 *The Bangladesh Labour Code 2006, Sec 218 (7).*
66 *Ibid, Sec 118 (13).*
67 *Ibid, Sec 218 (11).*
68 *Ibid, Sec 218 (13).*
69 Halim, Md. Abdul, *Textbook on Bangladesh Labour Code,* 8th Edition, CCB Foundation, Dhaka, 2017, p. 287.
70 *The State Acquisition and Tenancy Act 1950, Sec 145A (2).*
71 Hoque, Kazi Ebadul, *Administration of Justice in Bangladesh,* 1st Edition, Asiatic Society of Bangladesh, Dhaka, 2003, p.53.
72 *The State Acquisition and Tenancy Act 1950, Sec 145B (1).*

limits of jurisdiction regarding any Land Survey Appellate Tribunal. [73] Government shall appoint the judge of the land Survey Appellate Tribunal from amongst persons who are or have been judges of the High Court Division of the Supreme Court.[74] According to 145C of the State Acquisition and Tenancy Act, 1950 states that appeal against the order or decision of the tribunal lies before the Appellate Division of the Supreme Court if leave to appeal is granted.[75]

The Arbitration Tribunal:

According to the section 11 of the Arbitration Act, 2001, the parties shall be free to determine the number of arbitration and under the provision of this Act the parties are able to consist of arbitration tribunals. According to the provision of sec. 12 of the Arbitration Act 2001 parties may be appointed arbitrator to follow the requirement of the arbitration under this Act. According to the provision of sec 17 of the Arbitration Act 2001 provided that if the party is disagreed then the tribunal may exercise its own jurisdiction-

1. There is existence of a valid Arbitration agreement.
2. The arbitration tribunal is properly constituted for mediation.
3. Whether the arbitration agreement against the public policy
4. The arbitration is unable to preformed
5. What matter have been submitted to arbitration is accordance with the arbitration of agreement.

VAT Appellate Tribunal

Under Customs Act 1969, an Appellate Tribunal is established to be called the Customs, Excise and VAT Appellate Tribunal.[76] It consists of many technical and judicial members as it necessary.[77] Technical member shall be a person who was or is a member of Board or Commissioner of Customs and the person who has held any equivalent post for at least two years.[78] A judicial member shall be a person who has at least ten (10) years' experience as a judicial officer acted in District and Session Judges in Bangladesh, or who has acted as a Bangladesh Civil Service (Judicial) for at least three years or who has practiced as an

---

[73] *Ibid, Sec 145B (2).*
[74] *Ibid, Sec 145B (3).*
[75] Hasan, Mohammad Ikbal, *A Text Book On Land Law,* 1st Edition, Sui Juris, Chittagong, 2015, p. 274.
[76] *The Custom Act 1969, Sec 196.*
[77] Halim, Md. Abdul, *The Legal System of Bangladesh,* 8th Edition, CCB Foundation, Dhaka, 2014, p. 144.
[78] *Ibid, pp. 144-145.*

advocate for at least ten (10) years in not lawyer than the court of district and session judges court.[79]

It is a quasi-judicial body.[80] The Commissioner of Custom or other party may make an application of appeal to High Court Division within ninety (90) days from the date of serving notice.[81] In appellate Division, leave to appeal may be lodge regarding custom.[82]

Taxes Appellate Tribunal

It consists of a president and judicial and accountant members as the government thinks fit.[83] A judicial member shall be a person who, is or has been a District Judge, has practiced as an advocate in a court not lower than District & Session for a period not less than ten (10) years.[84] Appeal from Appellate Joint Commissioner or Commissioner lies to the Appellate Tribunal.[85] Appeal from Appellate Tribunal of Tax lies to the Appellate Division but with the certificate of High Court Division.[86]

Family Court:

Family courts have been established under the Family Court Ordinance 1985 (Now it is replaced by the Family Court Act, 2022) .[87] The assistant judge is the judicial officer of this court.[88] The court have jurisdiction over the following matters.[89]

1. Desolation of marriage
2. Dower
3. Restitution of conjugal rights
4. Maintenance
5. Guardianship and custody of children.

---

[79] *Ibid, p. 145.*
[80] *The Custom Act 1969, Sec 196C.*
[81] *The Custom Act 1969, Sec 196B.*
[82] Halim, Md. Abdul, *The Legal System of Bangladesh,* 8th Edition, CCB Foundation, Dhaka, 2014, p. 144.
[83] *The Income Tax Ordinance 1984, Sec 11.*
[84] *Ibid.*
[85] *Ibid, Sec 158.*
[86] *Ibid, Sec 160.*
[87] *The Family Courts Ordinance 1985, Sec 4.*
[88] Akkas, Sarkar Ali, *Independence and Accountability of Judiciary: A Critical Review,* 1st Edition, Centre for Rights and Governance, Dhaka, 2004, p. 97.
[89] *The Family Courts Ordinance 1985, Sec 5.*

The Court follows pre-trial proceeding and post-trial proceeding.[90] After filing written statement, the court shall fix a date within 30 days from filing written statement for a pre-trial hearing.[91] On the fixed date, the court will try to reconciliation and reach a compromise between parties on the disputed issues.[92] If the Parties don't agree to make a compromise between than the court shall pronounced its judgment[93] Where a disputes is settled by the conciliation or compromise, the court shall pronounced the decree or decision which is made by parties through conciliation or arbitration.[94]

Small Causes Court:

According to sec 25 of the Civil Courts Act 1887 small cause court was established for the settlement of small and petty claims matters between parties. There is no separate court for small cause but some regular judges, the joint district judge, senior assistant judge and assistant judge have jurisdiction to try cases of small cases. According to the section 15 of the Civil Courts Act 1887 all suits of civil nature of which values do not exceed 25 thousand taka shall be cognizable by the court of small causes and it is the highest pecuniary jurisdiction of this court. According to the sec 25 of the Civil Courts Act 1887,

1. Small causes suit valued up to taka six thousand is to be field in the court of assistant judge.
2. Suit valuation up to taka 10 thousand to be filed in the senior assistant judge court of the local area.
3. Suit valuation up to taka 20 thousand is to be filed is the joint district judge court of the local area vested with small causes lower.

No court shall try a suit which is cognizable by a small courses court. Because, section 15 of CPC states that every suit shall be instituted in the court of the lowest grade competent to try it. It shall follow the summary procedure and there is no need to follow the procedure of framing of issues & record of evidence.[95] Appeal from this court shall lie to the district judges' court.[96] High Court Division is empowered to revise the decision of small causes court.[97] District Judge Court shall control the small causes Court under the supervision

[90] Halim, Md. Abdul, *The Legal System of Bangladesh,* 8th Edition, CCB Foundation, Dhaka, 2014, pp. 156-157.
[91] *The Family Courts Ordinance 1985, Sec 10.*
[92] *Ibid.*
[93] *The Family Courts Ordinance 1985, Sec 13(2).*
[94] *Ibid, Sec 14.*
[95] *The Code of Civil Procedure 1908, Order 50.*
[96] *The Code of Civil Procedure 1908, Sec 104 & The Small Causes Court Act 1887, Sec 24.*
[97] *The Small Causes Court Act 1887, Sec 25.*

of High Court Division.[98] District Judge is empowered to withdraw a case from the small causes Court.[99] Small Causes Court have no jurisdiction in following matters;

- ✓ Execution of decrees.
- ✓ Execution of immovable property
- ✓ Attachment of immovable property
- ✓ Injunctions
- ✓ Appointment of receiver of immovable property

1.2.2c Criminal Courts

Criminal courts are those courts which try offences enshrined in the criminal laws existing in Bangladesh with a view to protecting and enforcing citizens' rights and upholding the rule of law in the society. Under the Code of Criminal Procedure, 1898 (hereinafter as CrPC) there shall be two classes of Criminal Courts in Bangladesh besides the Supreme Court and the Courts constituted under any law, namely: -

(a) Courts of Sessions; and

(b) Courts of Magistrates;

Magistrate court is of two types, namely:-

(a) Judicial Magistrate; and

(b) Executive Magistrate

Courts of Session Judge

In every district there is a Court of Session. A Court of Session is headed by the Session Judge, Additional Session Judge, Assistant Session Judge and they are appointed from District Judge, Additional District Judge & Joint District Judge. District judges shall have power to work as a Court of Session it has jurisdiction to give death sentence to confirm by, the High Court Division. When the Court of Session is situated in a metropolitan area is called the court of the metropolitan session. In has following types of jurisdiction

---

[98] *Ibid, Sec 28.*
[99] *Ibid, Sec 28A.*

i) Original jurisdiction.

ii) Appellate jurisdiction

iii) Revisional jurisdiction

iv) Jurisdiction as to transfer or with draw a case.

The Court can try fresh cases regarding criminal offence under Penal Code, 1860 or any other laws. In these cases, Colum 8 of Schedule II of the Code of Criminal Procedure, 1898 specify the offences which can be tried by Session Judge. The offences are waging, attempt to wage, war against Bangladesh, sedition, murder, culpable homicide, giving false evidence to cause a capital punishment, voluntarily causing hurt etc.[100]

Appeal from Additional Session Judge, District Magistrate, Additional District Magistrate, First Class Magistrate is laid before Session Court to hear and determine the appeal. Appeal from any sentence for up to 5 years by the Additional Session Judge or, any sentence for sedition charged under section 124A of the Penal Code, 1860 is laid before High Court Division in lieu of Session Court.[101] This court can't exercise appellate jurisdiction in such cases. The court is empowered to impose death sentence but subject to confirmation by the High Court Division. The Court is also authorized to exercise revisional jurisdiction on certain grounds, thus; sentence or order, legality, correctness, propriety of any finding, regularity of any proceeding before any inferior court.[102]

Court of Additional Session Judge:

The court of additional session judge shall exercise same powers like session judge court. When additional session judge situate in Metro Politian area is called additional metropolitan session judge. The court has no original jurisdiction, appellate jurisdiction and revisional jurisdiction but if the government direct or the Court of Session Judge transfer cases to deal as appeal, review or revision than it can try the cases.[103] It can pass death penalty.

---

[100] *The Code of Criminal Procedure 1898, Sec 28.*
[101] *Ibid, Sec 408.*
[102] *Ibid, Sec* 435.
[103] *The Code of Criminal Procedure 1898, Sec 193, 526 & 528.*

Court of Joint Session Judge:

Joint session judge may exercise any power authorize by law except a sentence of death or a term exceeding ten years imprisonment. When joint session judge located in metropolitan area is called joint metropolitan session court. It has also not original, appellate and revisional jurisdiction but if the government or Session Judge direct the Assistant Session Judge to try a case as appeal, review or revision, the court can exercise the functions.[104] It can't pass any death penalty.[105]

Judicial Magistrate Court:

According to section 6 (3) there shall be four types of judicial magistrate in district & metropolitan area namely:

(a) Chief Metropolitan Magistrate in Metropolitan Area and Chief Judicial Magistrate to other areas;

(b) Magistrate of the first class, who shall in Metropolitan area, be known as Metropolitan Magistrate;

(c) Magistrate of the second class; and

(d) Magistrate of the third class.

A Chief Metropolitan Magistrate and 1st Class Magistrate may try the offence provided in Schedule II of the Code of Criminal Procedure, 1898, thus; rioting, giving false evidence, sedition, assaulting or obstructing public servant during suppression riot, committing affray, bribery, voluntarily causing hurt, theft and other petty cases. A Chief Metropolitan Magistrate, Additional Chief Metropolitan Magistrate and other Metropolitan Magistrate are appointed to adjudicate criminal cases in a territory of Metropolitan. Government may with the consultation of High Court Division invest Chief Metropolitan Magistrate with power to try as a magistrate all offences not punishable with death.[106]

The Court of Magistrate may pass imprisonment for a term not exceeding five years and fine not exceeding ten thousand taka and whipping.[107] Section 29C of the Code of Criminal Procedure also empowered the court to pass any sentence

[104] *Ibid, Sec 139, 526B, 528.*
[105] *Ibid, Sec 31(3,4).*
[106] *Ibid, Sec 29C.*
[107] *Ibid, Sec* 32(1).

except death or imprisonment for terms exceeding seven years.[108] Outside the Metropolitan area, 1st Class Magistrate, 2nd Class Magistrate and 3rd Class Magistrate are appointed to try criminal cases. Magistrate of the First Class is also acted as Additional District Magistrate.[109] The Government may appoint more than one Magistrate of 1st Class, 2nd Class and 3rd Class in a district.[110]

2nd Class Magistrate:

According to the section 32 of the CrPC 2nd class magistrate may pass imprisonment up to 3 years including solitary confinement and give fine up to five thousand taka.

3rd Class Magistrate:

According to the section 32 of the CrPC 3rd class magistrate may pass imprisonment for a term not exceeding two years and fine not exceeding two thousand taka.[111] For the purpose of this sub section the world C.M.M. and C.J.M. shall include A.C.M.M. and A.C.J.M. respectively.

1.2.2d Special Criminal Courts

Nari-o-shisu nirjatan Daman Tribunal

Nari-o-shishu Nirjatan Domon Tribunal is established under the provision of the Nari-o-shishu Nirjatan Domon Ain 2000. According to the section 26 every district there must be a tribunal of such cases. If the government thinks necessary may consist of more tribunal in each district. The tribunal shall be consisted of by one judge who is appointed for amongst the district judge. It also includes Additional District Judge and Session Judge.[112] The Tribunal doesn't take any offence into cognizance without any report written by police officer not below the rank of sub-inspector or any person authorized by government.[113] Appeal from this Tribunal may be preferred to High Court Division within sixty days from the date of sentence, order and judgment of the Tribunal. Without confirmation of the High Court Division no death sentence can be executed.

---

[108] *Ibid, Sec* 29C.
[109] *Ibid, Sec* 10(1).
[110] *Ibid, Sec* 17(1).
[111] *The Code of Criminal Procedure 1898, Sec 32 (1,e).*
[112] *The Nari o Shishu Nirjatan Daman Ain 2000, 26 (4).*
[113] *Ibid, 27(1).*

The Speedy Trial Tribunal:

According to the Speedy Trial Act 2002 the government may be notification in the official gazette, may consist one more tribunal if he thinks fits and may notify the local limited of each tribunal the president may appoint as session judge on retired session judge of be the judge or special tribunal.[114] According to the section 5 of the speedy tribunal act the government may by notification of the official gazette may confer any offence to try this tribunal.

Ain-shirinkhula-bigno-kari-oporad (speedy try) Tribunal:

Ain- Shirinkhula – Bigno kari- oporad (Speedy Try) Ain-2002. The Govt. may by notification of the official gazette consist of one or more speedy trial tribunal. This tribunal is comprised with the first class magistrate. This tribunal shall try any offence under this ordinance.

The Environmental Court:

The environment court was established under section 4 of the Environment Court Act 2000 consisting at one judge hold post as joint district judge and it will be situated in every headquarters of the division. The government may appoint special magistrate to try any offence for which the punishment is not exceeding 2 years imprisonment and 10 thousand taka fine the offence mentioned in section 15 of this Act where the highest punishment is up to 10 year imprisonment and 10 lakh fine or both.

The Environmental Appellate Tribunal:

The Environmental Court Act 2000 provided the provision of established on environment appellate tribunal under section 12 comprising of a judge port of district judge. The government may empower a district and session judge to worth as a judge to the environment appellate court as an extra change and they will follow the proceeding of CRPC in criminal cases and proceeding toe CPC in civil case suit.

The Special Tribunal:

The special tribunal has been established under the Special Power Act 1974 with the session judge as special judge of the tribunal. It deals with the offence as special in the schedule of the act for offence punishable under the Special Power

---

[114] *The Speedy Trial Act 2000, Sec 4.*

Act 1974, The Arms Act 1818, and the Explosive Substances Act 1908. Rule made under the Emergency Power Act 1975, Section 376 of the Penal Code 1860 etc.

It consists with the Session Judge, Additional Session Judge and Joint Session Judge. Metropolitan or 1st Class Magistrate shall act as Additional Special Tribunal by the direction of government. It has empowered to transfer a case at any stage of the trial from one special tribunal to another special tribunal within same jurisdiction. (p. 152) Appeal form Special Tribunal may be filled before High Court Division within thirty days from the date of order.[115]

The Village Court

The village court consists of UP chairman, members and representatives from the concerned parties. Under the Village Court Act 2006, the village court can try disputes over property valued not exceeding TK. 3,00000. The village court has also power to summon a person to stand as a witness and can impose a fine of up to TK. 500 on contempt charges. The decision is drawn on the basis of majority. If the majority is four to one or three to one, the decision is final and there have no option to file an appeal. On the other hand, if the majority of three to two supports a decision, any party to the dispute may lie a revision application to the Assistant Judge in civil case and to the first class Magistrate in criminal case (sec. 8) No advocates are allowed to agree on behalf of parties. The pecuniary jurisdiction is till 5 thousand taka and the award by this court must not exceed taka five thousand.

1.3. Evaluation of Bangladesh Current Judiciary

The present judiciary are extremely suffering from huge backlog of cases; There are more than 4 million pending cases upon the present judiciary; consequently, people are not getting justice in due time and they are losing confidence upon the current judiciary; in some cases they declare openly that they have no confidence upon the judiciary and they don't want justice.[116] In some cases people wave their rights instead of bringing of a suit/ case due to not getting the justice in due time for very lengthy trial system and even they suicide due to not getting justice from any corner of the society.[117]. Even in some cases, the government is directly responsible for making the judiciary ineffective and for

[115] *The Special Tribunal Act 1974, 30 (2).*
[116] Khan, Sharier, Denying just won't do, *The Daily Star*, Dhaka, 2015, 2nd November, p.1
[117] Hasnat, Mahadi Al, Injustices drove Hazrat, daughter to suicide. *Dhaka Tribune*, 6th May, 2017. [accessed at 6.6.2018]. https://www.dhakatribune.com/bangladesh/2017/05/06/injustices-drove-hazrat-daughter-suicide

showing no confidence upon the judiciary rather extending helping hand to the judiciary by law enforcing agency in giving proper investigation report and bringing witnesses before courts at the trial of criminal cases and therefore, we see here continuous and random extra judicial killings by the law enforcing members and last update version of encounter doctrine for extra-judicial killing applying upon the suspected drug offenders and about 130 people have already reportedly been shot dead by security forces across the country[118] where even allegation has raised for killings of innocent people and a burning example of the killing of Teknaf municipality councilor Akramul Haque which was clearly revealed by the four audio clips from the victime's wife Ayesha Begum at a press conference at Cox's Bazar Press Club[119]. As a result, a culture of absence of justice has been created in the society. The current judiciary is failing to ensure justice in due time for many reasons: (1) exiting adversarial trial system which is very lengthy system (2) Backdated laws which having no application of digital system (3) inadequate of judicial officers [120] and office staff (4) inadequate accommodation (5) lack of proper court management (6) absence of separate investigation cell under the judiciary (7) Fake cases[121](8) malpractice by the parties and lawyers (9) corruption (10) interference from the executive etc.

Concluding Remarks:

Judiciary of Bangladesh comprises all courts and tribunals; it can broadly be divided into two categories: i) the lower judiciary & ii) the higher judiciary; the higher judiciary having two divisions- a) the High Court Division and b) the Appellate Division. The lower judiciary is of civil, criminal or special or tribunal. Civil courts are of: (1) The Court of the District Judge, (2) The Court of the Additional District Judge (3) The Court of the Joint District Judge, (4) The Court of the Senior Assistant Judge and (5) The Court of the Assistant Judge.

-Establishing ADR court as mandatory

Establishing people court for poor people where no court fees will be required and providing advocates to the clients

---

[118] Halt Killings of suspects in anti-drug drive, the Daily Star, Dhaka, 7th June, 2018, p.1

[119] Call for justice getting louder, the Daily Star, Dhaka, 6th June, 2018, p.1,2

[120] In comparing the number of judicial officers of other developed and developing countries in proportionate of their citizens, the numbers of judicial officers here are also very inadequate in proportion to our citizens. There are 18 judges in India, 107 in USA per 1 million citizens whereas here there are only 10 judges for the same number of citizens

[121] There is no accurate statistics on the status of false cases but it is often heard in the seminar, workshop from the concerned persons that 80% of total filing cases in the courts of the country are false. On 23rd June 2013 in seminar the former state law minister Quamrul Islam said that 80% lawsuits of the country are false (Progress Bangladesh, 2013).

Introducing Digital Application System in all cases

Increasing the number of judges and manpower

Ensuring adequate accommodation for smooth judicial functions

Establishing separate investigation cell under the judiciary

Introducing encouraging allowance for more disposal

Chapter 2:

Subordinate Judiciary and Citizens' Rights in Bangladesh[122]

Introduction

The judiciary in Bangladesh comprises all courts and tribunals which interpret law, settle legal disputes, enforce citizens' rights and impose penalty to the offenders and uphold the rule of law. In order to analyze the role of the Judiciary in Bangladesh it can broadly be divided into two categories: i) the subordinate judiciary (Lower Judiciary at District level) & ii) the higher judiciary; the higher judiciary having two divisions- a) the High Court Division and b) the Appellate Division (The constitution of Bangladesh, art.94 hereinafter as the Constitution). In this chapter, the role of lower judiciary in enforcing and protecting citizens' rights are examined by analyzing existing statutory laws, case laws and the number of disposal of cases by civil & criminal courts.

Lower judiciary refers to the subordinate courts-civil, criminal, special or tribunal etc. By the separation of judiciary from the executive in 2007, actually the magistrate courts are separated from the executive[123] and from that time these magistrate courts are termed as judicial magistrate courts and for that some changes have been brought in the Code of Criminal Procedure, 1908 (hereinafter as CrPC). Therefore, determination of the role of lower judiciary in the is matter of research and very important to evaluate the performance of the judiciary in discharging the responsibility protecting citizens' rights and upholding the rule of law. Generally, when citizens' legal rights special reference to life, property or legal protection are violated by individual private person or persons, they cannot seek the remedy by writ petition before the higher judiciary as the bar imposed by the Article 102(2) of the Constitution; they can go to civil courts or criminal courts for the protection and enforcement of the rights as the remedies are enshrined in the general laws. Besides, in several judicial pronouncements clear instructions have come on the point where the remedies lie as under:

---

[122] The author depends in conducting this chapter upon his PhD thesis titled 'Judiciary and Citizens Rights: Bangladesh Perspective (Not-Published) and the journal paper titled 'The Role of Subordinate Judiciary in Enforcing Citizens' Rights: Bangladesh Perspective. Int. J. Human Rights and Constitutional Studies, 2020, Vol. 7, No. 2, pp.85–99.

[123] All other courts of the country except magistrate courts were separate and independent before 2007; in the magistrate courts the preceding officers were executive magistrates under the supervision of the Deputy Commissioner or the Executive.

If the remedy sought for is available in the forum of civil court by a suit for specific performance of contract or for recovery of damages, aggrieved citizens should seek it in civil courts. Under this case, the extraordinary remedy by way of writ petition is not appropriate remedy (*Abdul Wadud v. AKM Nazmul Hossain* ,2009).

Generally private law remedies provided by the Code of Civil Procedure 1908 (hereinafter as CPC) and the Specific Relief Act, 1877(hereinafter as SR Act) are available for contractual rights disputes and the writ jurisdiction cannot be invoked for the enforcement of such rights *(Momin Motors Co. v RTA Dacca, 1962*).

There is no scope of writ court to decide any question of title *(Dewanbagh Darbar Sharif v. Bangladesh,* 2002). Therefore, where a citizen seeks the remedy-declaration of title, he has to seek it from the civil courts. Besides, the writ court will not decide a question in writ jurisdiction which is already pending in civil court *(Dr. M. O Ghani v. Dr. A.N.M. Mahmud,* 1996). Such court will not issue to question the claim to any office of a private association, institution, or college or school or a private corporation (Islam, 2012: p. 778-800). Under these cases, the aggrieved citizens can seek remedy from the lower judiciary. Under the heading –the role of lower judiciary, only civil courts and criminal courts especially judicial magistrate courts are taken into consideration for the evaluation of the role of the lower judiciary.

2.1. Civil Courts

Civil courts are those courts which have jurisdiction to try all suits of a civil nature, i. e. a suit in which the right to property, post or an office is contested except its cognizance is expressly or impliedly barred by any law (The Code of Civil Procedure, 1908, s.9) (Hereinafter as The CPC). Therefore, when citizens' individual legal rights or private rights e.g. right to property, post or office is affected, citizens can seek the remedies from the civil courts. There are five classes of civil courts recognized by the Civil Courts (Amendment) Act, 2001(Act No. XLIX of 2001) in Bangladesh, namely: (1) The Court of the District Judge, (2) The Court of the Additional District Judge (3) The Court of the Joint District Judge, (4) The Court of the Senior Assistant Judge and (5) The Court of the Assistant Judge. Among them, the District Court is subordinate to the High Court Division, and every Civil Court of a grade inferior to that of a District Court (CPC, Section 3). Besides, the Constitution declares that the High Court Division has superintendence and control over all courts and subordinate to it (The Constitution, a.109). The Court of Assistant Judge, the Senior Assistant Judge, and the Joint District Judge have original jurisdiction i.e. they can take a fresh suit and try it. The Court of the Additional District Judge has no original jurisdiction but the Court of the District Judge can take fresh suit in very few cases (e.g. disputes in trademark, patent, copyright etc.). The Assistant Judge Court can take any suit of value up to TK. 15, 00,000, the Senior Assistant Judge Court up to TK. 25, 00,000 from TK. 15, 00,001 and the Joint District Judge Court -TK. 25, 00,001 up to unlimited. It is the established rule that every suit shall be instituted in the Court of the lowest grade competent to try it (The CPC, s.15).

2.2 Ways to seek remedy in civil courts

When citizens' legal rights e.g. right to property, post or office is affected or denied by an individual or group of persons, aggrieved citizens can bring a civil suits in the civil courts. A civil suit is a suit where the right to property, post or office is contested. A citizen has to face broadly three stages in a civil suit: (a) Pre trial stages, (b) Trial Stages and (c) Post Trial Stages.

(a) *Pre-trial stages*

In the pre-trial stages a victim who seeks remedies from the civil court, has to face several steps. An aggrieved citizen who brings a suit in the civil court is known as plaintiff and against whom it is filed called as defendant. The steps in the pre-trial stage are: (i) presentation of plaint, (ii) summon, (iii) appearance of the defendants and filing of written statement, (iv) examination at first hearing / ADR, (v) framing issues, (vi) step under Section 30, and (vii) settling date (SD).

In order to bring a civil suit, the plaintiff has to present a plaint. Because of a civil suit is instituted by the presentation of a plaint.[124] The plaint is to be presented with *Vokalnama (*The CPC, s. 27 & Order V, r.1), proper documents papers upon which the plaintiff relies, the proper court fees and process fees.

'Summons' is an important step in a civil suit. It is to be issued upon the defendant to inform him that a suit has been filed against him, and that he is required to appear before the court to defend it (*Ibid*). The intimation which is sent to the defendant by the court is technically known as 'Summons'. Although the term 'Summons" has not been defined in the Code of Civil Procedure, 1908,

[124] CPC, 26; the word 'plaint' has not been defined in the Code of Civil Procedure though it directs that a suit shall be instituted by the presentation of plaint. Plaint is a written document in which the plaintiff asserts the facts, causes of action and claims relief.

it is a document issued from the office of a court of law. A summon can be issued upon the defendant/s in the four ways: (i) Personal Service, (ii) Service by affixation, (iii) Service by post, and (iv) Substituted Service.

If the summon is duly served upon the defendant, it is the duty of the defendant to appear before the court on the date fixed in the summons and defend the case by presenting a written statement; in case of his failure to submit it on that day, he will be allowed to file it another date but time for filing such a statement shall not exceed two months (*Ibid*, Order VIII, r. 1). It is apt to state that filing of written statement under CPC, Or. VIII, r. 1 is mandatory for the failure of which will be considered as admission of facts by the defendant (Haque, 2010:p.38). In the written statement, the defendant shall state his own case which he likes to prove against the case of the plaintiff. The defendant has to produce necessary documents accompanying with written statement to defence his case against the plaintiff claims (The CPC, Or. 8, rr. 1(2), (4) & (5).

After filing the written statement, the court shall take an initiative to mediate the dispute for alternative dispute resolution (popularly known as ADR) between the parties avoiding the formal procedure of litigation under section 89A of the Code of Civil Procedure.

If the ADR process fails, the court shall proceed from the mediation stage for first hearing. At this stage court will examine the pleadings of the parties and try to determine the core points of dispute between them.

At this stage, the court shall proceed to frame issues of the suit. Issue arises when material proposition of fact and law is affirmed by one party and denied by the other party (*Ibid*: p.45). The court frames the issues to arrive at a correct decision in a suit (*Ibid*).

After framing issues, the court may give order on application of the parties with regard to the delivery and answering of interrogatories, the admission of document and facts, and the discovery, inspection, production, impounding and return of documents or other material objects producible as evidence. After the step under section 30, CPC, the court settles a date for peremptory hearing that is date for trial.

(b) *Trial stage*

Opening the case is the 1st step of the trial stage of a civil suit. It is the right of the plaintiff to open the case and the plaintiff states the nature of the case, issue in the case, evidence of the witnesses. Then starts peremptory hearing (PH) where the plaintiff and defendant examine their own witnesses and cross-examine the witnesses of the adverse and may re-examine the witnesses (The Evidence Act, 1872, ss.137-138). After hearing the evidence of the witnesses of both parties the respective pleaders will be called upon to argue their case.

(c) *Post-trial stage*

Post-trial stage may consist of (i) pronouncement of judgment, (ii) decree/order and (iii) execution of decree. Once the hearing is complete, the court will pronounce judgment at once or reserve the judgment for future date. Every judgment contains (i) a concise statement of the case (ii) points for determination (iii) decision thereon (iv) reasons for decision. By the words of decree the court specifically determines and pronounces the rights of the parties in the pending dispute. Execution of the decree (if necessary) is the last stage of a civil proceeding and on the application of the decree holder, the court takes necessary step to execute the decree.

It is apt to mention that if a party is aggrieved by the decision of the trial court, he can file an appeal application before the Court of District Judge or the HCD; where the order is not appealable, in that case an aggrieved party can file an application for revision to the Court of District Judge against non-appealable orders of assistant judge court, senior assistant judge court and joint district judge court and revision lies to the HCD against non-appealable decrees of assistant judge court, senior assistant judge court and joint district judge court (The CPC, s.116).

2.3 Disposal of civil suits by the district civil courts

It is already mentioned earlier section that in case of infringement of individual civil rights by an individual or a group of individuals, an aggrieved citizen can file civil suits to district civil courts for seeking his remedy. And it is the onerous obligation of civil courts to provide remedies to the victims on the basis of law and evidence produced by parties. In order to investigate what performance was shown by district civil courts in the period (2008-2016), it is required to compare between filing and disposing of suits in the mentioned courts in yearly basis:

Table No.2.1: Number of Filing & Disposal of Suits in the District Civil Courts during the Period (2008-2016)

Year	Filing New Suits	Disposal of Suits	Remarks
2008	1,65,339	110,003	Disposal < Filing
2009	2,18,275	1,16,711	Disposal < Filing
2010	2,17,537	1,71,604	Disposal < Filing
2011	1,08,689	46,111	Disposal < Filing
2012	2,26,754	58,923	Disposal < Filing
2013	4,36,196	2,36,220	Disposal < Filing
2014	4,33,210	3,22,461	Disposal < Filing
2015	3,32,677	2,66,333	Disposal < Filing
2016	2,43,366	2,24,615	Disposal < Filing

Source: Annual Reports, 2008-2016, HCD, Supreme Court of Bangladesh

From the above comparative data upon the filing and disposing of suits in the districts civil courts, one thing is clearly revealed that the disposal rate is lesser than filing in each year from 2008 to 2016. This analysis is only between new filing and disposing of suits in the mentioned period. The pending cases of previous years particularly (1972-2007) were not considered. At the end of year-2007, there were 4, 56,604 suits pending for disposal which are of last 36 years before separation(HCD, Supreme Court of Bangladesh, Annual Report, 2008). In addition to these pending cases, new pending cases have also been added in each year in the period (2008-2016). And at the end of year-2016, pending suits stand as 12, 05,254 (*Ibid*, 2016). Therefore, new pending suits stand in this period as (12,05,254-4,56,604)=7,48,650 (Seven Lakh Forty Eight Thousand Six Hundred Fifty). The new pending cases in this period are almost thrice in comparing with pre-separation period (1972-2007). It is true if the statistics upon total filing number and disposal of suits is added here for last 36 years (pre-separation period), it would be better analysis and might get real picture which is only possible regarding writ matters discussed in the role of higher judiciary section.

2.4 Criminal Courts

Criminal courts are those courts which try offences enshrined in the criminal laws existing in Bangladesh with a view to protecting and enforcing citizens' rights and upholding the rule of law in the society. Under the Code of Criminal Procedure, 1898 (hereinafter as CrPC) there shall be two classes of Criminal Courts in Bangladesh besides the Supreme Court and the Courts constituted under any law, namely:- (a) Courts of Sessions ; and(b) Courts of Magistrates;

Magistrate court is of two types, namely:- (a) Judicial Magistrate; and (b) Executive Magistrate whereas Judicial Magistrate is of four types: (a) Chief Metropolitan Magistrate in Metropolitan Area and Chief judicial Magistrate to other areas; (b) Magistrate of the first class, who shall in Metropolitan area, be known as Metropolitan Magistrate; (c) Magistrate of the second class; and(d) Magistrate of the third class (The Code of Criminal Procedure, 1898 (hereinafter as CrPC), s.6). A Court of Session can try any offences under the Penal Code, 1860 and any other law mentioning no particular court in that law *(ibid*, ss.28 &29). A Sessions Judge or Additional Sessions Judge may pass any sentence authorized by law where only death sentence is subject to confirmation by the High Court Division and a Joint Sessions Judge may pass any sentence authorized by law, except a sentence of death or of transportation for a term exceeding ten years or of imprisonment for a term exceeding ten years *(ibid*, s.31). The Courts of Magistrates may pass sentences in the following ways: (a) Courts (of Metropolitan Magistrates and) of Magistrates of the first class: Imprisonment for a term not exceeding five years and fine not exceeding ten thousand taka; (b) Courts of Magistrates of the second class: Imprisonment for a term not exceeding three years, and Fine not exceeding five thousand taka; (c) Courts of Magistrates of the third class: Imprisonment for a term not exceeding two years and Fine not exceeding (two thousand taka) *(ibid*, s.32). Chief Metropolitan Magistrate (Chief Judicial Magistrate or any Additional Chief Judicial Magistrate) can try as a Magistrate all offences not punishable with death; Metropolitan Magistrate or any Magistrate of the first class with power to try as a Magistrate all offences not punishable with death or with transportation or with imprisonment for a term exceeding ten years *(ibid*, s.29C).

2.5. Ways to seek remedy from criminal courts or judicial magistrate courts

If a citizen is affected by the criminal activities of an individual or a group of persons, he can get remedy or seek justice from the criminal courts; and in these cases, he/she can lodge an FIR (First Information Report) in the Police Station for cognizable offences[125] or bring a complainant to the magistrate court in case of non-cognizable offences[126]. Even a citizen can bring a complainant to the judicial magistrate court for cognizable offences if he or she is failed to file a FIR at police station. The Magistrate having taken such complaint will examine the complainant upon oath under section 200, Cr.PC. Upon such examination

---

[125] Cognizable offences are such offences for which the police can arrest without warrant of judicial magistrate courts, viz. dacoity, murder, and robbery are examples of such offences.

[126] Non-Cognizable offences are such offences for which the police cannot arrest without warrant of judicial magistrate courts, viz. dishonor of cheque, fraud etc. are examples of such offences.

the Magistrate may take cognizance of the case or he may dismiss it or he may order for inquiry or investigation on the matter. Again, if any citizen files a FIR at the police station for non-cognizable offence, police cannot investigate upon this matter without the order of a magistrate; he can make a case entry in the General Diary and forward the informant to the magistrate for further steps (CrPC, ss. 155 &200). In a criminal case a victim faces broadly four steps: (a) Pre-Proceeding Stage, (b) Proceeding Stage, (c) Trail stage, and (iv) Post-trial Stage.

(a) ***Pre-proceeding stage***

In the *pre-proceeding stage* of a criminal case, police investigate the allegation against the accused and prepare a criminal case. Therefore, it can be said that in this stage police only play the role from the beginning to the end of this stage (Halim & Siddiki,2010: p.222). This stage includes the following steps:

(a) First Information Report (FIR) in cognizable offence
(b) Complaint in Non-Cognizable and Cognizable Offence
(c) Reporting to the Judicial Magistrate in case of PS Case[127], GR Case[128] and CR Case[129]
(d) Investigation & Maintaining Case Diary (CD)
(e) Final Report[130] or Charge Sheet[131]
(f) Final Report and *Naraji (*objectionable*)* Petition[132]

(b) Proceeding stage

In a criminal case, *proceeding stage* starts with taking of cognizance of the offences and issuing the process or summons. Here, any Chief Metropolitan Magistrate, Metropolitan Magistrate, Chief Judicial Magistrate, Magistrate of the first class, and any other Magistrate may take cognizance of any offence- (a) upon receiving a complaint of facts which constitute such offence; (b) upon a

---

[127] PS Case- Police Station (PS) Case- a case which is filed through an FIR in the police station, known as PS Case and a number is put against every FIR called as FIR No. or Police Station (PS) Case No… ….

[128] GR Case- General Registered Case (GR Case)-when the original copy of Police Station (PS) Case is sent without any delay to the Magistrate through the court officer as per requirement of section 157 of CrPC, he receives it and a number is put against the case is called General Registered Case (GR Case) and GR Case No……

[129] CR Case- Complaint Registered Case- When the Magistrate takes cognizance of a case upon the basis of a complaint brought by the affected citizen, it is registered as a Complaint Registered Case (CR Case)

[130] Final Report refers to a fact where police has not found no involvement of accused with commission of the offences brought against accused in FIR and under this circumstance, accused should be discharged from the allegation.

[131] Charge Sheet refers to a fact where in investigation police has found involvement of accused with commission of the offences brought against accused in FIR.

[132] If the Magistrate accepts the final report, the aggrieved informant can file a Naraji petition against it.

report in writing of such facts made by any police-officer; (c) upon information received from any person other than a police-officer, or upon his own knowledge or suspicion, that such offence has been committed (CrPC, s.190). Generally taking of cognizance of an offence is made in the presence of accused.

(c) Trial stage

After proceeding stage, the trial stage of a criminal case starts. Under the basis of nature of offences, punishment prescribed by law against them and the courts assigned by law to try them, a criminal case may be tried by either judicial magistrate courts or sessions judge courts. In case of trial by Judicial Magistrate Court the procedures which are followed as: (a) Pre-trial hearing/ Discharge before framing of charge (ibid, s.241A), (b) Framing of Charge (ibid, s.242) (c) Plea and conviction (ibid, s.243) (d) Taking Evidence where the accused does not make admission of commission of offence (ibid, s.244) (e) Examination of Accused under CrPC, section 342, (f) Final Arguments, (g) Judgment of Acquittal or Conviction. On the contrary, almost similar procedures are followed in trial by a court of session under CrPC, sections 265A-265L: (a) Opening case for prosecution(ibid, s.265B), (b) Discharge(ibid, s.265C), (c) Framing charge(ibid, s.265D), (d) Conviction of plea of guilty(ibid, s.265E), (f) Date for Prosecution Evidence(ibid, s.265F), (g) Evidence of Prosecution(ibid, s.265G), (h) Acquittal(ibid, s.265H)[133], (i) Entering upon accused defence(ibid, s.265I), (j) Arguments(ibid, s.265J), (k) Judgment of Acquittal or Conviction(ibid, s.265K).

(d) Post-Trial Stage

Post-Trial Stage refers to the execution of conviction and sentences. When the Court of Session passes sentence of death, the proceedings shall be submitted to the HCD for confirmation of death. In this case, the sentence shall not be executed unless it is confirmed by the HCD (ibid, s.374). Where the accused is sentenced to imprisonment, the Court passing the sentence shall forthwith forward a warrant to the jail in which he is, or is to be, confined, and, unless the accused is already confined in such jail, shall forward him to such jail, with the warrant (ibid, s.383). When a sentence has been fully executed, the officer executing it shall return the warrant to the Court from which it was issued, with

[133] Acquittal means exemption from the allegation after taking the evidence for the prosecution, examining the accused and hearing the prosecution and the defence on the point, the Court considering that there is no evidence that the accused committed the offence.

an endorsement under his hand certifying the manner in which the sentence has been executed (ibid, s.400).

2.6 Disposal of criminal cases by judicial magistrate courts

It is mentioned earlier that judicial magistrate courts have been separated from the executive since 1st Nov. 2007. Therefore, what performance has been shown by these courts in the period (2008-2016) is matter of research. In order to determine the role of the mentioned courts in the said period, it requires presenting a comparative yearly basis data on the number of filing and disposal cases in the mentioned courts:

Table No.2.2: Number of Filing & Disposal of Cases by the Judicial Magistrate Courts during the Period (2008-2016)

Year	Filing New Cases	Disposal of Cases	Remarks
2008	7,58,578	4,42,725	Disposal < Filing
2009	5,92,008	4,62,235	Disposal < Filing
2010	7,41,838	7,09,112	Disposal < Filing
2011	7,06,069	6,71,628	Disposal < Filing
2012	8,00,282	7,25,523	Disposal < Filing
2013	7,51,180	6,62,022	Disposal < Filing
2014	7,92,433	7,34,359	Disposal < Filing
2015	7,76,181	8,47,398	Disposal > Filing
2016	7,32,049	7,80,805	Disposal > Filing

Source: Annual Reports, 2008-2016, High Court Division, Supreme Court of Bangladesh

From the yearly basis comparative data on the number of filing and disposing of cases in magistrate courts, it is evident that disposal rate was lesser than filing of cases in first seven years (2008-2014) after separation whereas in the years 2015-2016, it is more than filing of cases. This data analysis is only between the number of filing and disposing of cases by judicial magistrates in the said period. In the end of year-2007, there were 6, 18,671 cases as pending in the magistrate courts (HCD, Annual Report, 2008). And the number of pending cases has also been increased in the separation subsequent years except 2015-2016 which creates a huge backlog of cases increasing suffering of litigants and hampering justice among the aggrieved citizens. In the beginning of the year-2008 the number of pending cases in the judicial magistrate was 6,18,178 (Six Lakh Eighteen Thousand One Hundred Seventy-Eight) but at the end of year-2016, the number of pending cases in the said courts has been increased and stood as

8,65,536 (Eight Lakh Sixty-Five Thousand Five Hundred Thirty-Six). As a result, new backlog of cases in this period stands as 2,46,865 (Two Lakh Forty-Six Thousand Eight Hundred Sixty-Five) (ibid, 2016).

Conclusion

The constitutional responsibility of Bangladesh Judiciary is to ensure, protect and enforce citizens' rights enshrined in the constitution and under ordinary laws. The lower judiciary is also assigned by general laws and the constitution to discharge its functions for enforcing citizens' non-fundamental or legal rights. Accordingly, the lower judiciary is serving its functions by providing judicial pronouncements on the basis of general laws, general principles and evidence of parties. It is true that the judiciary has shown its positive role in number of cases in the period (2008-2016) but the total disposal rate was lesser than filing of cases in the mentioned period except the disposal rate of cases in judicial magistrate courts for last two years (2015-2016) (see Table No. 1, 2). As a result, the number of pending cases has been increased rapidly in civil courts and judicial magistrate courts in the said period. At the end of year-2007 the pending cases were 4, 56,604 in civil courts, and 6,18,671 in magistrate courts whereas it stands as12,05,254 in civil courts, and 865536 in judicial magistrate courts respectively at the end of year-2016. This comparative data show that decree of overload or backlog of cases which is certainly increasing the suffering of right seekers and making linger of disposal of their cases. It is true that if total filing number of suits is found for last 36 years (pre-separation period), it might get real picture. Lastly, it can be said that in the research period the role of the Judiciary has strengthened more in protecting citizens' rights in Bangladesh. The separated courts specifically judicial magistrate courts have been increasingly discharging its responsibility; in the last years the disposal rate was higher than filing cases. But the Judiciary could dispose of more cases and play more important role if adequate number of judges were employed in the said period according to the proportionate of the people in Bangladesh in comparing with developing and developed country on the issue.[134]

[134] There are only 10 judges for per million people in Bangladesh where in India 18, in UK 51 and in Australia 41 as per Bangladesh Law Commission.

Chapter 3:

Higher Judiciary and Citizens' Rights in Bangladesh[135]

Introduction

The onerous responsibility of the Judiciary of a country is to ensure her citizens' rights if their rights are affected or taken away by the executive, legislature or any organ of the State, institution or law enforcement agency or even by individual/s. And Bangladesh Judiciary is also assigned same responsibility by the Constitution of the People's Republic of Bangladesh (hereinafter as the Constitution); in order to discharge such responsibility the Judiciary is empowered under Article 102 of the Constitution to examine the activities of the executive and review the laws passed by the legislature whether these laws are inconsistent with the provisions of fundamental rights enshrined in the Constitution and declare the inconsistent laws as void[136]. Under Article 44 of the Constitution, the High Court Division (hereinafter as the HCD) is declared as custodian to protect the citizen's fundamental rights enshrined in the third chapter of the Constitution. It is also held in the *Bangladesh v BLAST* [2016] 8 SCOB AD 1 that the Supreme Court is the custodian and protector of the fundamental rights of the citizens. In the case of Professor *Muhammad Yunus v Bangladesh* [2012] 64 DLR (AD)152 it was held that the power of HCD to issue writ under Article 102 can be exercised for the enforcement of fundamental rights as well as of non-fundamental legal rights where the action taken is procedurally ultra vires or where authority being an obligation to act judicially or even quasi-judicially, passes an order which is in violation of the principle natural justice, for safeguarding such fundamental rights of the aggrieved person. It is also opined in the case of *Khondoker Delwar v Italian Marble Works* [2010]62 DLR (AD) 298 that a citizen of Bangladesh is entitled to move the HCD under Article 102 for the enforcement of the rights conferred in Part III. It is apposite to mention that an aggrieved citizen can directly seek the remedy under Article 102(1) of the Constitution if his fundamental rights are infringed but in case of an application under Article 102(2) the petitioner must satisfy the

[135] The author depends in conducting this chapter upon his PhD thesis titled 'Judiciary and Citizens Rights: Bangladesh Perspective (Not-Published) and the published journal paper titled 'The Role of Higher Judiciary in Enforcing Citizens'Rights: Bangladesh Perspective', 2019, 5(4) International Journal of Law (IJL) p. 103- 111

[136] The Constitution of the People's Republic of Bangladesh (hereinafter as the Constitution), a. 26

court that there is no other equally efficacious remedy to his grievance.[137] If there is other equally efficacious remedy under general laws, the aggrieved citizens can seek remedies from the concerned authority declared by laws including district civil or criminal courts. Even the HCD cannot give relief to the citizens under article 102(2) if their rights are violated by a private individual. In that case, the subordinate courts can return the rights to the aggrieved citizens. Under article 102(2) the relief is only possible when the citizens' rights are violated by the Government or any of its authorities or any persons who exercising the public duties.

In the case of *Idrisur Rahman v Bangladesh* [2009] 61 DLR 523 the role of judiciary is described in the paragraph no. 208 as under:

> 'The judiciary stands between the people of the country and the State as a bulwark against Executive pressure, excesses and misuse of power by the Executive.'

In the above case, it is also cited that under the constitutional scheme, the Judiciary has been assigned the onerous task of safeguarding citizens' fundamental rights and upholding the rule of law[138].

In order to discharge the onerous responsibility of protecting and enforcing the rights of the citizens, the Judiciary must be independent, impartial and respected from all organs of the State and departments of the government. Bangladesh Judiciary (particularly judicial magistrate courts) has officially separated from the executive in 2007 by the consequence of landmark judgment known as *Masder Hossain's Case*. The higher judiciary- Supreme Court consisting of two branches High Court Division (hereinafter as HCD) and Appellate Division was separate and independent from the beginning of the birth of Bangladesh. More than 11 (Eleventh years) have gone from the formal separation of the judiciary. Within this period what role the higher has been performing in ensuring and protecting citizens' rights is a matter of research. With a view to gaining this objective the author has analyzed the existing laws and focused upon the comparative analysis of the filing and disposal rate of cases higher judiciary particularly writ benches and recent case laws in the period (2008-2016).

---

[137] *Concord Pragatee Consortium Ltd v BPDB* [2014] 66 DLR 475

[138] *Idrisur Rahman v Bangladesh* [2009] 61 DLR 523 Para.210

3.1. Higher Judiciary and Citizens' Rights

The judiciary in Bangladesh comprises all courts and tribunals which interpret law, settle legal disputes, enforce citizens' rights and impose penalty to the offenders and uphold the rule of law. In order to analyze the role of the Judiciary in Bangladesh it can broadly be divided into two categories: i) the subordinate judiciary (Lower Judiciary at District level) & ii) the higher judiciary; the higher judiciary having two divisions- a) the High Court Division and b) the Appellate Division.[139] The lower judiciary is of civil, criminal or special or tribunal. In this paper the role of higher judiciary in enforcing and protecting citizens' fundamental and non-fundamental legal rights are determined by analyzing existing statutory laws, case laws and the number of disposal of cases by writ petitions by the HCD during the period (2008 - 2016).

The Constitution empowers the HCD as custodian to protect the citizens' fundamental rights. [140] The same view was held in a recent judicial pronouncement that the Supreme Court is the custodian and protector of the fundamental rights of the citizens.[141] The HCD can grant necessary orders and reliefs for the enforcement of fundamental and non-fundamental rights under Article 102 of the Constitution. The HCD can also apply the power of judicial review conferred upon it by the Constitution to examine the activities of the executive and legislature with a view to ensuring citizens' rights and establishing the rule of law. An aggrieved citizen can seek the enforcement of his infringed fundamental rights in bringing a writ petition before the HCD.

Whenever the rights of a citizen are affected, it is the constitutional mandate upon the court to adjudicate it and enforce it. [142] If it finds that citizens' fundamental rights are infringed, it is the constitutional obligation of the HCD to pass orders for the enforcement of fundamental rights under Article 102(1) of the Constitution. Article 102 empowers the HCD to grant necessary orders and reliefs for the enforcement of fundamental and non-fundamental rights. Article 102(1) particularly confers power upon the HCD on the enforcement of citizens' fundamental rights but in the matter of enforcement of fundamental rights the aggrieved citizen generally has to apply before the HCD. On this point the Constitution declares as under[143]:

---

[139] The Constitution of Bangladesh, art. 94.

[140] *Id*, art. 44.

[141] Bangladesh & ors v BLAST & ors [2016] 8 SCOB AD 1.

[142] Mahmudul Islam, *Constitutional Law of Bangladesh* (3rd edn, Mullick Brother 2012).

[143] The Constitution of Bangladesh, art.102.

> The High Court Division on the application of any person aggrieved may give such directions or orders to any person or authority, including any person performing any function in connection with the affairs of the Republic, as may be appropriate for the enforcement of any of the fundamental rights conferred by Part III of this Constitution.'

It is apt to state here that the right to move to the HCD for the enforcement of fundamental rights under Article 44 of the Constitution is itself a fundamental right. A citizen should not wait for violation of a fundamental right; he can move to the HCD even when he faces a threat to his right.[144] Even a citizen can bring a petition before the Court under Article 102 for the enforcement of fundamental rights though his rights are not directly and personally affected; where his rights commonly or collectively affected; where the undetermined people are affected, where the undetermined persons are very poor, helpless; where there is public wrongs, injuries or invasion to the fundamental rights of undetermined number of people;[145]actually where a citizen is not personally affected but he is sufficiently interested with the matter in dispute;[146]when a public functionary owing to serve to the people in general but it is not served, the common interest of all citizens are affected and each citizen is deemed as aggrieved;[147] under these circumstances a citizen can bring an action before the HCD in the name of 'public interest litigation'. In the case of *Ekushey Television Ltd.* v *Dr. Chowdhury Mahmood Hasan* (2003) 55 DLR (AD) 26, para 34 observed:

> The nature of the public interest litigation (called PIL hereinafter) is completely different from traditional case which is adversarial in nature whereas PIL is intended to vindicate rights of the people. In such a case benefit will be derived by large number of people in a contrast to a few. PIL considers the interest of others and therefore, the court in public interest litigation acts as the guardian of all the people whereas in a private case the court does not have such power. Therefore, in public interest litigation the court will lean to protect the interest of the general public and the rule of law vis-à-vis the private interest.

In connection to the PIL the Supreme Court held in *Kazi Mukhlesur Rahman* v *Bangladesh* (1974) 26 DLR (AD) 44:

---

[144] *Id.* art. 44

[145] *Dr. Mohuuddin Farooque v Bangladesh* [1997] 49 DLR (AD)1.

[146] *Nasiruddin* v *Secretary, LGRD* [1999]51 DLR (AD) 213.

[147] *Mrs. Parvin Akter v Rajuk,* [1998]18 BLD 117, para 15.

> Public interest litigation means the legal action initiated in a court of law for the enforcement of rights and interest of citizens in general or a section thereof. The judiciary is to play a vital and important role not only preventing and remedying abuse and misuse of power but also to eliminate injustice. It must not be forgotten that the cause of justice cannot be allowed to be thwarted by any procedural technicalities. An action may be maintained for judicial redress brought before it by a citizen provided from such action the State will be benefited.

In a public interest litigation, the right of a citizen is not directly or personally affected but he can take action on behalf of undetermined number of people if he has sufficient interest in the dispute matter; he will have *locus standi* if he initiates to vindicate the cause of the people in general or that of a group in the society who are for some reasons not in a position to vindicate their cause before the court. On the contrary, the court is under constitutional obligation to adjudicate the matter brought before it for ensuring and enforcing citizens' rights and establishing the rule of law. In case of public interest litigation, the court is under obligation to inquire the motive of the applicant whether the applicant brought it for bad intention or not before the court instead of affected people; if the motive is to serve the interest of somebody than the interest of common people, the court should declare that applicant has no *locus standi* though it is a public interest litigation.[148]

When a matter of infringement of a citizen's fundamental right is brought before the Court, it is the obligation of the Court to grant necessary reliefs but the decisions of the HCD are not final as the aggrieved citizen can appeal under the Constitution, Article 103; to grant relief for the enforcement of citizens' fundamental rights is not discretionary of the Court but it is obligatory. In a case the Appellate Division (AD) gave an *obitur dictum* that when any violation of fundamental rights enshrined in the Constitution was alleged as the only ground and no violation of legal right or any provision of law protecting citizen's right was raised, only then resort may be taken to fundamental rights to protect any citizen of such right.[149] In case of clear and blatant violation of fundamental rights, the Court may grant compensation to the victim citizen.[150] In a recent leading case the HCD opined that the court is competent to award compensation for infringement of fundamental rights by colourable exercise of power by

[148] The Constitution of Bangladesh, art. 102.
[149] *Chairman RAJUK v Abdur Rouf Chowdhury* [2009] 61 DLR (AD) 28.
[150] The Constitution of Bangladesh, art. 102.

police under section 54 & 167 of the Code of Criminal Procedure.[151] In the mentioned case the detenu is directed to be set at liberty within three hours and the District Magistrate is to pay him a compensatory cost of Taka 5,000 for the whimsical exercise of power curtailing the liberty of a person.

3.2 Higher Judiciary: Fundamental and Non-Fundamental Legal Rights

The Constitution confers the power of judicial review under Article 102(2) upon the HCD to examine the activities of the executive and legislature with a view to ensuring citizens' rights and establishing the rule of law. The HCD may grant necessary orders on the application of an aggrieved citizen when his fundamental and non-fundamental rights are affected subject to exhaustion of alternative efficacious remedies available to him. It is also stated in earlier section that when any question of violation of fundamental rights raised as the only ground and no violation of legal right or any provision of law protecting citizen's right was alleged, only then resort may be taken to fundamental rights to protect any citizen of such right.[152] And in case of only violation of fundamental rights, the court grants remedies under Article 102(1) a of the Constitution and for violation of non-fundamental right or any provision of the constitution or provision of law protecting citizen's right, the remedies are available in Article 102(2) subject to the exhaustion of alternative efficacious remedies to him by any law. But in case of enforcement of fundamental rights under Article 102 (1), no need to exhaust the efficacious remedy and an application can be directly entertained by Article 102 (1).

An aggrieved citizen can seek remedies under Article 102(2) in the form of writ[153] petitions which is historically originated and developed in the British Legal System. It was exercised and issued by the Crown by virtue of prerogative and known as prerogative writs e.g. the writ of *habeas corpus*, *mandamus*, *prohibition*, *certiorari*, procedendo, and *quo-warranto*.

In Bangladesh, the Constitution empowers the HCD under Article 102 to issue the writs on the petitions made by the aggrieved citizens. It is apt to state that the term writ or different forms of writ are not directly used in the Constitution; they are used technically. If the language of article 102(2) is analyzed, five types of writ viz. the writ of *habeas corpus*, *mandamus*, *prohibition*, *certiorari*, and *quo-*

---

[151] *Korban v Bangladesh* [2003]55 DLR 194.

[152] *Chairman RAJUK v Abdur Rouf Chowdhury* [2009] 61 DLR (AD) 28.

[153] A writ literally means a written order. It refers a written command, precept, or formal order issued by a court, directing or enjoying the person or persons to whom it is addressed to do or refrain from doing some act specified therein.

warranto are found which the High Court Division may, on the application of any person aggrieved, make an order in response as under:

1. directing a person performing any functions in connection with the affairs of the Republic or of a local authority ---- this order refers as writ of *mandamus;*[154]
2. to refrain from doing that which he is not permitted by law to do or to do that which he is required by law to do---- this order is writ of *prohibition;*[155]
3. declaring that any act done or proceeding taken by a person performing functions in connection with the affairs of the Republic or of a local authority, has been done or taken without lawful authority and is of no legal effect---- this order is known as writ of *certiorari;*[156]
4. directing that a person in custody be brought before it so that it may satisfy itself that he is not being held in custody without lawful authority or in an unlawful manner---- this order is writ of *habeas corpus;*[157] and
5. requiring a person holding or purporting to hold a public office to show under what authority he claims to hold that office---- this order is writ of *quo-warranto.*[158]

i. *Writ of Mandamus*

Mandamus means 'we command'. By this writ the higher judiciary directs a person holding office of a public nature to do something, which he is bound by law but abstains from doing. Article 102(2)(a)(i) of the Constitution empowers the HCD to issue a writ of mandamus to compel a person performing functions in connection with the affairs of the Republic or of local authority. But this article does not require that the applicant for mandamus must have a specific legal right; it only requires the applicant to be an aggrieved citizen.[159] It may issue where there is a violation of legal right or of legal duty by a person performing functions in connection with the affairs of the Republic or of local authority.

---

[154] The Constitution, a. 102(2)(a)(i).
[155] *ibid.*
[156] *ibid*, a. 102(2)(a)(ii).
[157] *ibid*, a. 102(2)(b)(i).
[158] *ibid*, a. 102(2)(b)(ii).
[159] Supra Note 8.

Mandamus may issue on the government for the following purposes established by the judicial pronouncements:

a) to take necessary measurements to prevent adulteration of food;[160]
b) to direct the governmental authority in taking steps for installation of speed governor in in all the public transports to ensure safety of the people;[161]
c) to establish vacation court in every district;[162]
d) to compel the government to hold the commission for inquiry into violation of human rights;[163]
e) to direct police to prosecute an offender against law or
f) to record FIR start investigation;[164]
g) to pay leave salary, allowance, or future salary;
h) to restore seniority of a government servant, or
i) to direct the government to realize arrear telephone bills from the members of the parliament etc.

No mandamus can issue to give direction for implementation of recommendation or decision of inter-ministerial correspondence in writ jurisdiction due to inter-ministerial communications being as merely policy guidelines but not creating any rights.[165]Such writ cannot be issued to compel the government to implement its policy nor can it be issued merely on consideration of equity.[166]Nor mandamus can issue for restoration to office in Private Corporation.[167]

ii. *Writ of Prohibition*

Prohibition means 'to forbid' from doing something. Article 102(2)(a)(i) of the Constitution confers the power to the HCD to issue a writ of prohibition. Such writ can issue where a tribunal proceeds to act (a) without or in excess of jurisdiction, (b) in contravention of some statute or the principles of common law, (c) in violation of principles of natural justice, (d) under a law in which

---

160 *Human Rights for Peace for Bangladesh v Bangladesh*, 2010 BLD 125.
161 *Bangladesh v Ministry of Home Affairs* [2008]16 BLT 264.
162 *Monzil Morshed v Bangladesh* [2008]16 BLT 327.
163 *Asaduzzaman v Bangladesh*, 2009 BLD 643.
164 *Hasuba Begum v Ministry of Home Affairs*, 2010 BLD 481.
165 *Aminullah v Bangladesh* [2008] 13 BLC 224.
166 *Md. Abdul Bari v Bangladesh* 2010 BLD 465.
167 *Shahidul Islam v Bangladesh* [2008] 60 DLR 710.

itself is ultra vires or unconstitutional, or (e) in contravention of fundamental rights. Such writ also lies against judicial and quasi-judicial bodies.[168]

iii. *Writ of Certiorari*

Certiorari means 'be certified' of the proceedings of any lower court or tribunal to be investigated by the superior court. Article 102(2)(a)(ii) of the Constitution empowers the HCD to issue writ of certiorari with a view to declaring an act done or proceeding taken by a person performing functions in connection with the affairs of the Republic or of a local authority to be without lawful authority and of no legal effect. Simply stating that the HCD can interfere when the person proceeded against has done an act without lawful authority. But this article does not permit the HCD to interfere on the ground of error of law on the face of record.[169] Under Article 102(2)(a)(ii) of the Constitution, an order can be passed against any authority, irrespective of the nature of the function, if he is performing the function in connection with the affairs of the Republic or any local authority.

iv. *Writ of Habeas Corpus*

Habeas Corpus means 'have his body' i.e.to have the body before the Court. Article 102(2)(b)(i) of the Constitution provides to the HCD the power and obligation to issue a writ in the nature of habeas corpus when a citizen is detained without any lawful authority and in an unlawful manner.[170]Such writ is available against any wrongful detention whether by a public functionary or by a private person.[171] It lies against all illegal detention by public functionaries involve infringement of fundamental rights guaranteed in Articles 31-33 of the Constitution. It is also maintainable against a private individual when the question of illegal custody is involved.[172]A habeas corpus proceeding is not maintainable if the person concerned has been released. Such writ will not be maintainable where the detention order has been passed but the person concerned has not been detained.[173]

---

[168] The Constitution, art. 102.
[169] *ibid.*
[170] *Dr. Shipra v Bangladesh* (2009)14 BLC 561.
[171] The Constitution of the People's Republic of Bangladesh, art. 102.
[172] *Bangladesh Jatiyo Mahila Ainjibi Samity (BJMAS) v Ministry of Home Affairs and Others*, 2008 BLD, 580.
[173] *Mohammad Ali v BD* [1995] 47 DLR 350.

v. Writ of Quo Warranto

Quo Warranto means 'by what warrant or authority'. Article 102(2)(b)(ii) confers the power upon the HCD to issue the writ of quo warranto requiring a person holding or purporting to hold a public office to show under what authority he claims to hold that office. Such writ will lie against speaker, chief justice or a judge of the HCD, ministers, members of parliament, chairman of municipality, members of the municipal board, administrator of municipal corporation appointment by the government, chief engineer of Municipal board, member of bar council, chairman or member of union parishad, member of senate or syndicate of a university, Dean of a faculty in a university, Chief Metropolitan Magistrate, government pleader or against the members of civil service.[174]

In order to bring a petition under Article 102(1) & 102(2) (a) of the Constitution a citizen must be aggrieved one. And Article 102(2) requires that an affected citizen must exhaust the alternative efficacious remedy available before him. Therefore, it is relevant to explain in reference to judicial pronouncements who is an aggrieved person and whether he exhausts the alternative efficacious remedy available before him before made the petition before the HCD under the said article:

(a)*Aggrieved person*

Article 102 requires that the petitioner seeking enforcement of fundamental rights or constitutional remedies must be a person aggrieved.[175]The Constitution does not define the terms. The terms are defined in several judicial pronouncements. In case of *Nasiruddin* v *Secretary, LGRD* (1999)51 DLR (AD) 213 it was observed that the aggrieved person means a person who even without being personally affected has sufficient interest in the matter in dispute. When a public functionary owing to serve to the people in general but it is not served, the common interest of all citizens are affected and each citizen is deemed as aggrieved.[176]Under Article 102(2) an application for mandamus, prohibition or certiorari are required to be brought by aggrieved persons but under the same article viz. Article 102(2)(ii) of the Constitution, the applicant does not require to be an aggrieved one in bringing a writ for *quo warranto*.[177]

---

[174] The Constitution, art. 102.
[175] *Bangladesh Sangbadpatra Parishad v Bangladesh* [1991] 43 DLR (AD) 126.
[176] *Mrs. Parvin Akter v Rajuk*, (1998) 18 BLD 117, Para.15.
[177] *Bangladesh v Md. Aftabuddin*, 2010 BLD (AD) 1.

Any person may apply where the public interest is related with the matter.[178] For the same reason, an application for habeas corpus can also be made by any person who needs not be a 'person aggrieved'. It is pertinent to state here that for the enforcement of all fundamental rights the application has to be filed by an aggrieved person and apparently when the detention of a person is challenged as violative of fundamental rights guaranteed under Article 32 or 33 of the Constitution, the application has to be filed by an aggrieved person. On the contrary, any person can file a writ petition if violation of fundamental right is not alleged or involved.[179]

(b) *Exhaustion of efficacious remedy*

The rule of exhaustion of alternative remedies is a rule of the court where it requires that in order to entertain writ petitions; an affected citizen has to satisfy the court that he/she exhausted the alternative efficacious remedies. Under Article 102 (2) of the Constitution, it is a requirement that the applicant has to exhaust efficacious remedy available to him by any law in order to make an application before the HCD for judicial review of any action taken by a person holding office of a pubic nature whereas in case of enforcement of fundamental rights under Article 102 (1), no need to exhaust the efficacious remedy and an application can be directly entertained before the Court. Under Article 102(2) of the Constitution, writ will be maintainable for enforcement of non-fundamental rights subject to exhaustion of statutory remedies. Better explanation was established in several judicial pronouncements. As for examples, thus when a contract incorporates provision of arbitration, writ will not lie in respect of such contract for non-exhaustion of the remedy provided in the contract; the petitioner can take recourse to resolution of the dispute by arbitration.[180]If there is any illegality in convicting a person, the remedy is by way of appeal or revision provided by the statute and not by way of writ. But where there is no provision of appeal or revision for illegal conviction, the detenu may bring it before the HCD in the form of writ.[181] Where there is special provision for appeal against judgment and decree of the Artha Rin Adalat, no writ petition lies under Article 102 maintainable unless the judgment is without jurisdiction.[182] Where it is claimed by the petitioner that he has executed an enforceable

[178] The Constitution, art. 102.
[179] *Id.*
[180] *Nazrul Islam v Bangladesh* [2006] 58 DLR 431.
[181] *Rajab Ali v East Pakistan* [1958] 10 DLR 385.
[182] *Edruk Ltd v Bangladesh* [2009] 14 BLC 102.

agreement, his relief lies in a suit of lower judiciary for specific performance and not in writ jurisdiction.[183]

3.3. Disposal of Writs by the Courts

It is earlier stated that if the fundamental rights or even non-fundamental rights of citizens (subject to exhaustion of efficacious alternative remedy) are infringed by the State herself or any governmental institutions or law enforcement agencies or government employees while discharging their duties, the aggrieved citizens can seek enforcement of their rights through the writ petitions from the HCD under Article 102(1) & (2) of the Constitution. Therefore, it is the research question what performance has been shown by the higher judiciary in regards enforcement of citizens' rights? In doing so, a yearly based data in the period (2008-2016) regarding filing and disposal of writs by Writ Courts are analyzed:

Table No.3.1: Number of Filing and Disposal of Writs by Writ Courts

Year	Filing New writs	Disposal of Writs	Remarks
2008	11,402	8915	Disposal < Filing
2009	8,848	6370	Disposal < Filing
2010	10,175	7303	Disposal < Filing
2011	11,421	10924	Disposal < Filing
2012	17,876	8028	Disposal < Filing
2013	12,958	7473	Disposal < Filing
2014	12843	8688	Disposal < Filing
2015	14,284	13457	Disposal < Filing
2016	16,965	9857	Disposal < Filing

Source: Annual Reports, 2008-2016, HCD, Supreme Court of Bangladesh

From the above yearly basis comparative data, one thing is revealed that the number of disposal of writs is lesser than number of filing writs in each year particularly from the year-2008 to year- 2016. This analysis was confined only between new filing and disposing of writs in the mentioned period. In the previous years (1972-2007) 126,175 writs were instituted but among them 86024 writs were disposed of. As a result, in the said period, 40,151 writs were pending for disposal where Supreme Court Annual Report 2016 reveals that at the end of year-2007, total pending writs has stood as 40,980 (Forty Thousand Nine Hundred Eighty). In contrary, in the period (2008-2016)116472 writs were filed but only 81015 writs were disposed of. Accordingly, in this period new

[183] *Abdul Wadud v Nazmul Hossain* [2009] 14 BLC 14.

35457 writs stand as pending. However, if consider total pending writs column of Supreme Court Annual Report 2016, the total number of pending writs stand as 69,326 (Sixty-Nine Thousand Three Hundred Twenty-Six) at the end of year-2016. Therefore, in the period (2008-2016) new pending writs stand as (69326-40980) =28346 (Twenty-Eight Thousand Three Hundred Forty-Six). The scenario can be conveniently shown in figure as under:

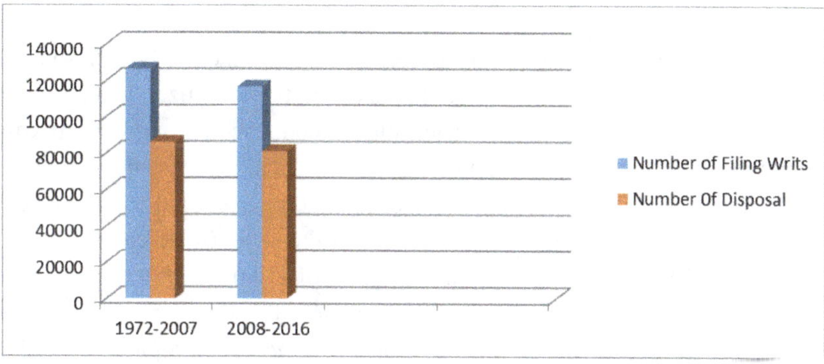

In the pre-separation period (1972-2008), on an average 3505 writs were filed and about 2390 writs were disposed of per year whereas in the research period 12941 writs were filed and 9558 writs were disposed of per year. In the pre-separation period total judges of the High Court Division including writ benches was 1117 and on an average there were 31 judges per year whereas in the research period total judge was 815 and about 91 judges per year.[184] As a result, it is revealed that in the research period the filing and pending rate of writs, both per year were thrice where the number of judges was thrice but disposal rate per year was four fold in comparing with the pre-separation period (1972-2008). Therefore, the disposal rate was increased in the research period in comparing with the pre-separation period (1972-2008).

3.4 Citizens' Rights: Case Laws and Case Study

The onerous responsibility of the judiciary is to protect and enforce citizens' rights and upgrade the rule of law. And judiciary is discharging such functions by exercising its extraordinary power –judicial review for the examination of the functions of the government or its different organs or any persons involved with public functions. The relevant cases discharged by the Judiciary in the period (2008-2016) have been selected and studied in order to determine the role of judiciary in enforcing citizens' rights as under:

[184] Annual Report,2016, HCD, Supreme Court of Bangladesh.

In the case of Professor *Muhammad Yunus v Bangladesh* [2012] 64 DLR (AD)152 it was held that the power of HCD to issue writ under Article 102 can be exercised for the enforcement of fundamental rights as well as of non-fundamental legal rights where the action taken is procedurally ultra vires or where authority being an obligation to act judicially or even quasi-judicially, passes an order which is in violation of the principle natural justice, for safeguarding such fundamental rights of the aggrieved person.

It is now well settled proposition of law that even the HCD can sou moto interfere when it comes to its knowledge that liberty of a citizen had been taken away by the unlawful ground. In such matter court should avoid technicality. When the State does not raise any objection in such circumstances, this court can certainly interfere, when the liberty of a citizen is curtailed and his valuable right of freedom is taken away by the order of the subordinate court. The HCD is empowered under section 491 of the Code of Criminal procedure to set at liberty of the victim who is found to be detained illegally or improperly. Such observation was given in the case of *Emran Ahmed v Bangladesh* [2012] 64 DLR 462

On the contrary, it is held in the case of *Khondoker Delwar v Italian Marble Works* [2010] 62 DLR (AD) 298 that a citizen of Bangladesh is entitled to move the HCD under Article 102 for the enforcement of the rights conferred in Part III. This substitution of article 44, no doubt, was designed to advance the rule of law and the welfare of the people and accordingly it needs to be retained for the interest of justice.

In the case of *Siddique Ahmed v Government of Bangladesh and others* [2013] 65 DLR (AD) 08 it is held that since the vires of Section 3 of the Constitution (Seventh Amendment) Act 1986, was as issue, the writ petitioner rightly invoked the extraordinary powers of the High Court Division. Since no equally efficacious remedy is provided under any other provisions of law, the persons who are aggrieved by the orders of the Martial Law Courts, may in appropriate cases, invoke the extraordinary powers of the High Court Division.

In the case of *RAJUK v A Rouf Chowdhury* [2009] 61 DLR (AD) 28 it was decided that when any violation of fundamental right enumerated in the Constitution was alleged as the only ground and no violation of legal right or law has been alleged whatsoever without reference to the provision of law protecting the right of a citizen, only the resort may be taken to fundamental right to protect any citizen of such rights.

In the case of *Mahbubul Alam v Bangladesh* [2009] 61 DLR 728 it was decided that a person in the service of the Republic who intends to invoke fundamental right for challenging the vires of a law will seek his remedy under Article 102(1) but in all other cases he will be required to seek remedy under Art. 117(2) of the Constitution.

In the case of *Bangladesh Biman Corporation and others v Md. Zahangir Farazi and others* [2013] 65 DLR (AD) 116 it was held that once the inter-ministerial /divisional communications or departmental notes are given effect to by way of communication and the parties, so communicated act on that, a legal right is accrued to them and if that right is infringed or is threatened to be infringed them they may approach a Court of law to protect such right.

In case of *Concord Pragatee Consortium Ltd v BPDB* (2014) 66 DLR 475 it was held that the fundamental difference between two sub-articles of Article 102 of the Constitution is that while Article 102 (1) can be invoked directly if an aggrieved person can make out a case of infringement of fundamental rights, however, in order to qualify to be an applicant under Article 102(2), the aggrieved person must satisfy the court that there is no other equally efficacious remedy to his grievance.

Jurisdiction under Article 102(2), as a whole, is known as an extraordinary jurisdiction and the same is to be availed of only when there is 'no other equally efficacious remedy' available.

It restricts access to judicial review by inserting the terms "if no other equally efficacious remedy is provided by law". With the peculiar jurisdictional restrictions the Supreme Court of Bangladesh did not lag far behind in its bid to reach justice to the poor and the underprivileged in times of their need.[185]

It is also held in case of *Golzar Hosain (Md), Advocate v Janata Bank* [2013] 65 DLR (AD) 101 that the power of judicial review under Article 102 cannot be invoked unless it can be shown that the alterative remedy is not efficacious or adequate, the wrong complained of is inextricable mixed up and the vires of the statute or a statutory provision is challenged.

In the case of *BLAST v Bangladesh* [2011] 63 DLR the fact is that the news which were published in different dailies on the imposition of extra judicial punishment by the name of Fatawa across the country upon the women and men

---

[185] *Maulana Syed Rezaul Haque Chadpuri v Bangladesh Jamaat-e-Islam* (Spl Original) 66 DLR (2014) 14.

in the form of lashing and beating, which are violative of fundamental rights guaranteed in the Constitution under Articles 31, 32, and 35 have been brought in the form of writ partitions before the court by the petitioners namely BLAST, BMP, ASK, BRAC and Nijera Kori to declare the imposition and execution of extra judicial punishment by the name of Fatawa as illegal and violative of fundamental rights and to give directions the respondents to take necessary steps to stop and prevent them. Some news of them is as under:

The petitioners came to know from a report published in "The Daily Prothom Alo" on 24. 5.2009 that a woman of Naogaon village, Daudkhandi Upazila, Comilla had to face 39 lashes by the village elders' salish (arbitration) due to born a child out of wedlock. In consequence of lashes the woman was seriously wounded and was admitted into the Daudkhandi Upazila Complex Hospital.

Another report in the Daily Star on 16.8.2009 titled "Fatwa Again" 101 lashes for refusing uncle's sexual advances" stated that a woman was whipped in public following issuance of a Fatwa by a local muezzin.

One report published in the Daily Star on 24.1.2010 under the heading "Village Arbitration- Rapist spared, victim lashed" is a fact of writ petition; a girl of 16 years had to receive 101 lashes in the name of Fatwa after 8 months being raped in Kasba Upazila by village arbitration but amazingly no punishment is given to the rapist, Enamul Mia, 20 years.

Another report was published in the Daily Prothom Alo on 22. 5.2010 where the fact is that the victim had an affair with a hindu boy. A village arbitration consisting of the village elders, and three imams gave order 101 lashes on the victim as per Islami Sharia. The uncle of the victim carried out the lashing of 101 dorra (lashes) and one stage, the victim became unconscious.

In the mentioned case, under the above circumstances, the court declared the imposition and execution of extra judicial punishment by the name of Fatawa as void, having no legal effect without proper lawful authority and violative of fundamental rights enshrined in the Constitution. The Court also gave some directions to be implemented by the government to prevent the imposition and execution of extra judicial punishment by the name of Fatawa from the society.

In the case of *HRPB v Bangladesh* [2011] 63 DLR the petitioner, Human Rights and Peace for Bangladesh is a non-profit organization which works (a) to uphold the human rights of the citizens, (b) to work for the poor people (c) to give legal support to the helpless people, (d) to work for the protection of the life of the citizens and (e) to build up the awareness amongst the people about their rights. Reports were published in the daily newspapers that Bangladesh is on the risk of earthquake zone, which created threat to the life of the people of the country. So, proper steps to save the life of the citizens are of great public importance and it is the first duty of the state to take proper steps to save the life of the citizens but the governmental authority has yet taken any steps to collect proper equipment to face earthquake even after the continuous news reported in the daily newspapers. The petitioners served a notice on the respondents to take necessary steps including adequate preparation and arranging rescue equipment. And therefore, the petitioner filed the instant writ petition before the court and obtained the Rule Nisi. In this Rule Nisi asking the respondents to show cause as to why the inaction of the respondents to arrange sufficient equipment in the natural disaster in consequence of earthquake should not be declared to be illegal and without lawful authority and why a direction should not be given upon the respondents to arrange sufficient rescue equipment to save the life of the citizens in case of the earthquake.

It is opined by the Court that the government is bound to protect life and property of the people in the discharge of its constitutional obligation; the Government has been directed to make available sufficient necessary equipment for rescue of the citizens soon after occurrence of a severe earthquake. And it is also declared that recent news items published in different national dailies creates great anxiety among the citizens of Bangladesh. Even it is also declared that if further direction is needed, the parties will be at liberty to make applications in the instant rule as this rule nisi will be treated as continuous mandamus.

In the case of *BELA v Bangladesh* [2010] 62 DLR 463 the petitioner, Bangladesh Environmental Lawyers Association (BELA) brought a writ petition under Article 102 of the Constitution to direct the respondents to protect the river Jadukanta (in the mouzas of Puranlaur, Chaliarghat, Lamasram, Purbadoil and Ghagra, Police Station- Thairpur, Distrct-Sunamganj) from the illegal extraction of sands from its bed and banks and to give further directions to initiate legal measures against the illegal and unscrupulous and traders and also to realize compensation from them for causing damages to the river and the villagers of the said villages. The petitioner stated in the petition that the environment and ecology of the country are being continuously endangered and threatened by various activities originating from the public and private affairs.

The rivers of Bangladesh were affected largely and the people surrounding it are fallen into the problems and their rights are being violated as a consequence. This scenery is reflected in case of the river Jadukanta. From the immemorial time, the lives of the people of Sunamganj are very closely connected to this river and its resources but due to illegal extraction of sands from the bed of this river the lives of the people are at stake. The surrounding villagers of this river always claim proper management, maintenance and protection of this rivers but the concerned authority fails to do so. Therefore, the matters were brought before the HCD in the form of writ petition. In this case the court recognized the right of the villagers under Articles 31, 32, 42 of the Constitution in the following ways:

> Right to protection of law, to life and to hold properties of the villagers are guaranteed by the Constitution and the respondents are duty bound to discharge their duties to ensure those rights of the villagers. This is a fit case for giving direction upon the respondents to stop illegal extraction of sand from the bed and banks of the river and outside the designated area of the Fazilpur Sand Quarry.

Finally, the court has granted remedies sought by the petitioners and gave directions to the concerned authority to protect the river from illegal extraction of sand from its bed and banks and thus to protect the constitutional rights of the villagers.

In the case of *Bangladesh Beverage v Rowshan Akter* [2010] 62 DLR 483 the deceased Mozammel Hossain Montu was husband of the plaintiff-respondent, reporter of Daily Sangbad. He met accidental death on 3.12.1989 consequence of fatal injuries (injured on the head, face and skull was totally broken) at the time of crossing the road in front of Ananda Bhaban, Shantinagar by the minibus of the defendant-appellant being No. Dhaka 6933, rushing from the eastern side-Jonaki Cinema Hall (i.e. coming from wrong side). At the time of the death, the deceased was only about 44 years leaving 2 minor sons, parents, brother, sister, and wife. The Plaintiff-respondent, wife of the deceased brought the claims of TK. 3, 52, 97000 as compensation before the court. The lower court gave judgment on behalf of the plaintiff and the HCD also gave decree to the plaintiff on 11th May, 2010. The defendant-appellant is directed to pay TK. 2,01,47,008 as compensation. And the Court also had shown its anxiety over regular accidental death of the citizens in the Country. The court has shown its anxiety as following ways and gave recognition to the right of life to the citizens:

> Life is bundle of incident. Every child is born with expectation of life and with constitutional guaranteed right of basic requirements for living. Death is inevitable but premature death in whatever form is not expected and cannot be consoled. Accidental death is also a premature death. Government is answerable to all such premature death as Government is to protect the citizen and is responsible for the life of a citizen.

In the case of *Emdadul Haque v DG, Education* [2008] 60 DLR the petitioner is a demonstrator of computer studies in the intermediate level of the Shyampur Degee College, Rangpur. He got appointment letter on 6.12.2003 and joined on 11-12-2003. In September, 2005, he was enlisted in the MPO list and continuously received MPO portion of salary till April, 2008. However, from May, 2008 his name was withdrawn from the MPO list without any notice and he filed a representation to the concerned authority but got no satisfactory reply. By this circumstance, he was compelled to bring a writ petition before the HCD to seek his right. The Court gave decision on behalf of him; the withdrawal of the name of the petitioner from the MPO list without giving any notice and affording an opportunity of being heard to the petitioner is a clear violation of the principle of natural justice; the withdrawal of the name of the petitioner from MPO list has been declared as made or done without any lawful authority and is of no legal effect; the respondents was directed to pay the petitioner the MPO salary from May, 2008.

Conclusion

The constitutional responsibility of Bangladesh Judiciary is to ensure, protect and enforce citizens' rights enshrined in the constitution and under ordinary laws. The higher judiciary of Bangladesh particularly the High Court Division of the Supreme Court of Bangladesh is discharging its responsibility by examining the activities of the government and by reviewing the laws passed by the legislature whether it is inconsistent with provisions of fundamental rights enshrined in the constitution. It works as custodian and protector of the fundamental rights of the citizens. Such positive role has been found in number of judicial pronouncements of the Supreme Court of Bangladesh in the recent years particularly in the period (2008-2016) (which is already discussed in sections 3 & 4). In a recent judicial pronouncement, it is held that the court can certainly interfere when the liberty & the freedom of right of a citizen is taken away by the subordinate court. It is also held that by the section 491 the HCD is empowered to declare liberty of the victim if he/she is found to be detained illegally or improperly.[186]In another case, the court declared the imposition and execution of extra judicial punishment by the name of Fatawa as void, having no legal effect without proper lawful authority and violative of fundamental rights enshrined in the Constitution. The Court also gave some directions to prevent the imposition and execution of extra judicial punishment by the name of Fatawa from the society. [187] In another judicial pronouncement, the higher judiciary declared corporeal punishment viz. caning, beating, and chaining upon children in various educational institutions as absolutely prohibited, inflicting it be deemed as misconduct of the concerned teachers, and gave directions to the concerned authorities of the Government to take necessary steps to prevent the imposition of corporeal punishment by way of framing and adopting and disseminating appropriate guidelines, directions or orders to all concerned authorities.[188] It is true that the judiciary has shown its positive role in number of cases in the period (2008-2016) but the total disposal rate was lesser than filing of cases in the mentioned period (see Table No. 3.1). As a result, the number of pending cases has been increased rapidly in in writ courts in the said period. At the end of year-2007 the pending cases were 40,980 in writ courts whereas it as 69,326 in writ courts at the end of year-2016. This comparative data show that decree of overload or backlog of cases which is certainly increasing the suffering of right seekers and making linger of disposal of their cases. It is also found that in the research period the filing and pending rate of writs in the writ courts were thrice per year where the number of judges was also thrice but disposal rate was four folds per year in comparing with the pre-separation period (1972-2008). Therefore, the disposal rate was increased in the research period in comparing with the pre-separation period (1972-2008). As a result, it can be said that in the research period the role of the Judiciary has been strengthened more in protecting citizens' rights in Bangladesh. The Judiciary could dispose of more cases and play more important role if adequate number of judges were employed in the said period according to proportionate of the people in Bangladesh in comparing with developing and developed country on the issue.[189]

[186] *Emran Ahmed v Bangladesh* [2012] 64 DLR 462.

[187] *BLAST v Bangladesh* [2011] 63 DLR 1.

[188] *BLAST v Bangladesh* [2011] 63 DLR 643.

[189] There are only 10 judges for per million people in Bangladesh where in India 18, in UK 51 and in Australia 41 as per Bangladesh Law Commission.

Chapter 4:
The Separation of Judiciary in Bangladesh-Constitutional Mandates and *Masdar Hossain Case's* Directions[190]

Introduction

Separation of judiciary is an important principle of an effective judiciary. Without separation of the judiciary, the independence of judiciary is not possible and if the judiciary is not independent, then the citizen's rights, it may presume, may be violated; rule of law is not possible to be established. It is observed in *Second Judges'* case[191] (1998) 7 SCC 739 that "so long as the Judiciary remains truly distinct from both, the Legislature and the Executive, the general power of the people can never be endangered from the any quarters".

State has three important organs- executive, judiciary and legislative. Among them, judiciary is very important to ensure citizens' constitutional rights, legal rights if their rights are infringed either by the executive or legislature or by any department or institution of the government or even by an individual or a group of individuals. It is rightly said that "the judiciary stands between the people of the country and the State as a bulwark against Executive pressure, excesses and misuse of power by the Executive" (61 DLR 523, Para- 208). Therefore, the judiciary of a country must be separate, independent and competent. The concept of separation of the judiciary from other organs of a State refers to a situation in which the judicial branch of government acts as its own body free from intervention and influences from the other branches of government, particularly from the executive and Legislature.

In Bangladesh, the separation of Judiciary and its independence are the constitutional mandates as they incorporated in several articles [192] of the Constitution of the People's Republic of Bangladesh (Hereinafter as the Constitution) : Article 22 of the Constitution provides that "the State shall

---

[190] The author depends in conducting this chapter upon his PhD thesis titled 'Judiciary and Citizens Rights: Bangladesh Perspective (Not-Published) and the published journal paper titled 'Separation of Judiciary in Bangladesh-Constitutional Mandates and Masdar Hossain Case's Directions: A Post Separation Evaluation' International Journal for Court Administration, 2020, 11 (2), pp.1-20.

[191] Cited in *Idrisur Rahman* v. *Bangladesh* (2009) 61 DLR 523.

[192] See the Constitution, arts. 22, 94, 109, 116A

ensure the separation of the judiciary[193] from the executive organs of the State" whereas Article 94(4) of the Constitution states that "the chief justice and the other judges of the Supreme Court[194] of Bangladesh shall be independent in the exercise of their judicial functions." The same view is also reflected in the article 116A [195] regarding the judges [196] and judicial magistrates [197] of the subordinate courts. Even, in the case of *Secretary, Ministry of Finance v. Masder Hossain and others*[198], (hereinafter as the *Masdar Hossain* judgment) it was opined upon the provisions of the independence of the judiciary affirmed in the Article 94(4) and Article 116A as one of the basic pillars of the Constitution which could not abridged, curtailed or diminished in any manner.[199] On the contrary, Article 109 provides that the High Court Division (hereafter as HCD) of the Supreme Court of Bangladesh (hereinafter as SCB) shall have superintendence and control over all courts and tribunals subordinate to it. If the

---

[193] The judiciary of a country comprises all courts and tribunals which interpret law, settle legal disputes, enforce rights of citizens and impose penalty to the offenders. The Judiciary of Bangladesh can be drawn broadly by the Supreme Court (higher judiciary) and subordinate courts (lower judiciary). The highest court in Bangladesh is known as the Supreme Court of Bangladesh having two divisions- a) the High Court Division and b) the Appellate Division (Bangladesh Constitution, Art. 94) (hereinafter as the Constitution). Subordinate courts may be civil, criminal, special or tribunal.

[194] The highest court in Bangladesh is known as the Supreme Court of Bangladesh

[195] Article 116A reads as: "Subject to provisions of the Constitution, all persons employed in the judicial service and all magistrates shall be independent in the exercise of their judicial functions".

[196] The term judges refer to the District Judges, Additional District Judges, Joint District Judges, Senior Assistant Judges and Assistant Judges; they are presiding officers of the Subordinate Civil Court (Lower Judiciary) at the District Level of Bangladesh.

[197] Judicial magistrate means the presiding officers of subordinate criminal courts (lower judiciary in BD) at the District level; they take cognizance of offences and try criminal matters under the Code of Criminal Procedure (CrPC), 1908.

[198] 52 DLR (AD) 82, Para. 57.

[199] The same view first established in the case of *Anwar Hossain Chowdhury v. Bangladesh* 1989 BLD (Spl) 1(8th Amendment Case); where it was held that the basic features or structures of the Constitution being not altered or changed in any way; of which separation of powers incorporated in Article 22 of the constitution and the independence of the judiciary inserted as in the Articles 94(4) and 116A are two important basic structures ; *subsequently*, the same views came in the following cases: *The State v Chief Editor, Manabjamin,*)57 DLR 2005 HCD 359, *Abdul Mannan Khan* v. *Bangladesh* (2012) 64 DLR 169, AKM *Shafiuddin v. Bangladesh* (2012) 64 DLR 508, 16th Amendment case (Civil Appeal No.06 of 2017) available at: http://www.supremecourt.gov.bd/resources/documents/1082040_C.A.6of17.pdf (Last visited on 31 August 2018), Mobile Court Case 2017 (writ no. 8437 & 10482 of 2011, and 4879 of 2012) available at: www.supremecourt.gov.bd/resources/documents/382548_WP8437of2011.pdf (Last visited on 25 June 2018). It is apt to state that the doctrine of the basic structure is an Indian judicial principle that the constitution has some basic features cannot be changed, altered or destroyed by the amendments of the legislature. The principle was first established in 1964 in the case of *Sajjan Singh v. State of Rajastan*, (1965) AIR 845, SCR (1) 933 cited in Wikipedia, Basic structure doctrine available at: https://en.wikipedia.org/wiki/Basic_structure_doctrine (Last visited on 4 September 2018). In the different judicial pronouncements of Indian judiciary, constitutional matters are now settled matters that constitutional supremacy, fundamental rights, State directive principles, rule of law, judicial review, separation of powers etc. falling in the category of constitutional basic features. On the contrary, in Bangladesh after several judicial pronouncements, the legislature has incorporated the provisions of basic features of the Constitution in the Constitution (Article 7B) by Article 7 of the Constitution (Fifteenth Amendment) Act, 2011 (Act XIV of 2011) where the preamble, all articles of Part I (Provisions regarding the Republic), Part II (Provisions regarding Fundamental Principles of State Policy), Part III (Provisions regarding Fundamental Rights), and Article 150 of the Constitution are clearly declared as basic structures of the Constitution which shall not be amendable by way of insertion, modification, substitution, repeal or by any other means; See the Constitution of the People's Republic of Bangladesh available at: http://bdlaws.minlaw.gov.bd/print_sections_all.php?id=367(Last visited on September 5, 2018).

higher judiciary has control and superintendence exclusively upon the subordinate judiciary, the independence of the subordinate judiciary is possible to be established. In the *Masdar Hossain* judgment, the institutional independence of the subordinate judiciary, especially from the Legislative and the Executive has been treated as third essential condition of judicial independence.[200]Even in 1972's Constitution, the SCB got priority in case of controlling and supervising of the subordinate judiciary due to the provisions of original Articles 115 and 116 where Article 116 empowered the SCB to control over the subordinate judiciary in case of postings, promotions, grant of leave and discipline and under Article 115, district judges would be appointed by the President on the Supreme Court's (hereinafter as SC) recommendation but current articles 115 & 116 empowered the President in place of the SC.[201]

It was very unfortunate for the nation in spite of having mandatory provisions regarding the separation of the judiciary in the Constitution, 1972, no effective steps were ever taken by the legislature or executive or any government in order to separate the judiciary from other two branches before 2007. And finally, it was officially separated from the executive on the 1st November, 2007 by the then caretaker- government in order to meet such constitutional mandates and the directions of the Appellate Division given in the case of *Secretary, Ministry of Finance* v. *Masdar Hossain and others*[202] 20 BLD (AD) 141; the underlying purpose is to establish the rule of law and uphold the citizens' rights; in the mentioned case the Appellate Division gave twelve directions, of which five was mandatory and seven was optional.

By the separation declaration on 1st November, 2007, the subordinate judiciary particularly judicial magistrate courts[203] were separated from the executive but effective separation is yet to be established. Under these circumstances, whether all directions of *Masdar Hossain's* judgment have been implemented? If they all

---

[200] *Secretary, Ministry of Finance v. Masdar Hossain and others,* 52 DLR (AD) 82, Para. 62.

[201] Current Articles 115 and 116 have created a real obstacle to a meaningful and effective separation and independence of the judiciary as these two articles have empowered the President to make appointments of judges and judicial magistrates of the lower judiciary and to deal with posting, promotion, discipline of judicial officers in consultation with the Supreme Court. Actually, these two articles give the executive absolute control over the lower judiciary where original Article 115 was substituted by section 19, the Constitution (Fourth Amendment) Act, 1975 and Article 116 substituted by the Constitution (Fifteenth Amendment) Act, 2011.

[202] Popularly Known as judiciary separation case

[203] Judicial magistrate courts are now part of the subordinate judiciary, take cognizance of offences and try criminal matters under the Code of Criminal Procedure (CrPC), 1908; Under the CrPC, magistrate court is now of two types, namely:- (a) Judicial Magistrate; and (b) Executive Magistrate; Before 2007's separation there were only magistrates courts held by the executive; now four types of Judicial Magistrate operates under CrPC: (a) Chief Metropolitan Magistrate in Metropolitan Area and Chief judicial Magistrate to other areas; (b) Magistrate of the first class, who shall in Metropolitan area, be known as Metropolitan Magistrate; (c) Magistrate of the second class; and(d) Magistrate of the third class (CrPC, s. 6); such magistrate courts were not existed before 2007's separation rather magistrate courts held by the executive magistrates were working.

are implemented whether true separation of judiciary is established here? or what are the reasons behind for the non-establishment of true separation of the judiciary in Bangladesh? These are all the research questions of the current chapter. By applying analytical research methodology, this chapter is conducted.

A great deal of literature has been written upon the separation of power and separation of the judiciary. Literature regarding separation of judiciary after 2007 will be considered here as the research area is regarding post separation period of the Judiciary. In Bangladesh targeted literatures particularly research based works upon the post separation of judiciary is hardly available. Justice Latifur Rahman agreed in a judicial pronouncement for financial independence for effective and meaningful discharge of the constitutional functions of the judiciary which might ensure its effective separation[204]. Dr. Zahidul (2012) claimed that the judgment of the *Masdar Hossain* case remained largely unimplemented until 2006; he determined many inconsistent with the independence of judiciary in Bangladesh, particularly, controversial appointments to the High Court Division (hereinafter as HCD), appointment of Chief Justice(hereinafter as CJ), appointment of public prosecutors, arbitrariness in judicial actions, withdrawal of cases on political ground, the manner of refusal of bail to political leaders and arbitrary presidential pardon etc., for which questions raised among citizens regarding separation of judiciary and its independence[205]. M Rafiqul (2014) argued for the absence of due process of law and justice in the activities of the executive giving opportunity to the executive body great deal of interest making the separation of judiciary at stake[206]. He also identified that the maintenance of a dependable judiciary has created a political expedient for the executive which is also a bar for ensuring separation of judiciary. Huda (2017) claimed for effective separation of the administration of justice from the legislative and executive power for the preservation of the public liberty where the appointment of the judges by the executive is a great restraint for effective separation.[207] Shakhawat (2018) claimed that meaningful

---

[204] *Secretary, Ministry of Finance v. Masdar Hossain and others,* 52 DLR (AD) 82, Para. 89.

[205] Dr. Zahidul Islam Biswas, "Do We Have an Independent Judiciary?", 6 (9) *Forum the Daily Star (Dhaka, September, 2012)* available at : https://works.bepress.com/zahid/8/download/ (Last visited on August 13, 2018).

[206] M Rafiqul Islam, "Independence of the Judiciary-the Masdar Case" *The Daily Star* (Dhaka, 10th March 2014) available at: https://www.thedailystar.net/opinion/straight-line/independent-judiciary-must-democracy-1381690 (Last visited on August 13, 2018)

[207] Muhammad Nurul Huda, "Independent Judiciary a must for democracy" *The Daily Star* (Dhaka, 27 March 2017) available at: https://www.thedailystar.net/opinion/straight-line/independent-judiciary-must-democracy-1381690 (Last visited on 13 August 2018).

and effective judiciary was not possible in 45 years due to collective failure of the executive, legislature and the judiciary.[208]

4.1 Separation of Power: Historical Background

Separation of powers, an idea became visible at the time of Montesquieu and even before.[209] The concept of separation of powers derived from centuries of political and philosophical development[210] reflected first in Aristotle's book *The Politics.*[211] In this book, the author focused three elements or powers of a government where first element is the deliberative element pertaining to common dealings like as war and peace, enactment of laws, penalty of death, appointment, confiscation and deportation.[212] Second element refers to the number of offices and subject matter of its dealing as well as the tenure of offices.[213] And third element is the component part of judiciary which denotes the system of court, element of judiciary, appointment procedure of judges and structure of court.[214] The third element of the government merely touches the doctrine of separation of powers.

Later on, in 1690, Locke in his *Second Treatise of Civil Government* focused about the independence of judiciary and the theory of separation of powers saying that 'it is necessary there should be a power always in being which should see to the execution of the laws that are made, and remain in force. And thus the legislative and executive power comes often to be separated'.[215] It is also stated that: 'The executive and federative power of every community be really distinct in themselves, yet they are hardly to be separated and placed at the same time in the hands of distinct persons. The executive and federative power should be placed in persons that might act separately, whereby the force

---

[208] Shakhawat Liton, "A Collective Failure" *The Daily Star* (Dhaka, 9th January 2018) available at: https://www.thedailystar.net/frontpage/collective-failure-1517050 (Last visited on August 13, 2018).

[209] Jr. Laurence J O'Toole, "Doctrines and Developments: Separation of Powers, the Politics-Administration Dichotomy, and the Rise of the Administrative State" 47 (1) *PAR* 17-25(1987) available at: http://www.jstor.org/stable/975468?seq=1&cid=pdf-reference#references_tab_contents (Last visited on May 27, 2018).

[210] Sam J. Ervin, JR., "Separation of Powers: Judicial Independence" 30 *LCP* 108-127(1970) available at: https://scholarship.law.duke.edu/lcp/vol35/iss1/8 (Last visited on November 25, 2018).

[211] Benjamin Jowett, *Aristotle's Politics* 175-176 (Translated Version), Book IV, Part, XIV *(*Oxford University Press 1920) available at: https://ia800503.us.archive.org/7/items/aristotlespolit00aris/aristotlespolit00aris_bw.pdf (Last visited on May 31, 2018).

[212] *Id.*

[213] H Reckham, *Aristotle Politic*s 385 (English translated version) (Harvard University Press, Cambridge 1959) available at: https://ryanfb.github.io/loebolus-data/L264.pdf (Last visited on May 31, 2018).

[214] *Id.*

[215] John Locke, *Two Treaties of Government* 168 (New edn, Vol. 5, 1823, Para 144 available at: https://www.yorku.ca/comninel/courses/3025pdf/Locke.pdf (Last visited on May 31, 2018).

of the public would be under different commands, which would be apt some time or other to cause disorder and ruin.'[216]

In 1748, Great French Philosopher Montesquieu formulated the doctrine of separation of powers in his famous book *The Spirit of the Laws* stating that:

> 'In every government there are three sorts of power: the legislative; the executive in respect to things dependent on the law of nations; and the executive in regard to matters that depend on the civil law. By virtue of the first, the prince or magistrate enacts temporary or perpetual laws, and amends or abrogates those that have been already enacted. By the second, he makes peace or war, sends or receives embassies, establishes the public security, and provides against invasions. By the third, he punishes criminals, or determines the disputes that arise between individuals. The latter we shall call the judiciary power, and the other, simply, the executive power of the state.'[217]

Montesquieu explicates that each power of the government's three organs should be exercised by each organ itself so that no apprehensions of interfering functions of the organs by each other can arise. He thus emphasized upon the separation judiciary:

> 'When legislative power is united with executive power in a single person or in a single body of the magistracy, there is no liberty, because one can fear that the same monarch or senate that makes tyrannical laws will execute them tyrannically. Nor is there liberty if the power of judging is not separate from legislative power and from executive power. If it were joined to legislative power, the power over the life and liberty of the citizens would be arbitrary, for the judge would be legislator. If it were joined to executive power, the judge could have the force of an oppressor.
>
> All would be lost if the same man or the same body of principal men, either of nobles, or of the people, exercised these three powers: that of

[216] *Secretary, Ministry of Finance v. Masdar Hossain and others,* 52 DLR (AD) 169 para 148.
[217] Baron De Montesquieu, *The Spirit of Laws* (translated into English by Thomas Nugent) (The Colonial Press, New York, vol. 1, 1899); cited also in George W. Carey, "Separation of Powers and the Madisonian Model: A Reply to the Critics" 72 *APSA* 154(1978) available at: http://www.jstor.org/stable/1953605> (Last visited on May 27, 2018).

making the laws, that of executing public resolutions, and that of judging the crimes or the disputes of individuals.'[218]

In 1824, William Paley who is the famous English philosopher and theologian observed about the doctrine of separation of power in his '*Moral and Political Philosophy'* as under: The judges of the land become not infrequently the arbitrators between the king and the people, on which account they ought to be independent of either; or, what is the same thing, equally dependent upon both; that is, if they be appointed by one, they should be removable only by the other.[219]

However, there are lots of criticisms against the doctrine of separation of power. Absolute separation of power of each branch is never possible and also not desirable; therefore, the subsequent doctrine introduced as check and balance among three organs where US is burning example to follow the most rigid check and balance among three organs where in Bangladesh the principle of check and balance is not ensured constitutionally and in practice; As a result, in spite of declaring the constitution as the supreme law of the country and ensuring constitutional supremacy, the executive and legislative are working as supreme organs in practice against which true separation and effective independence are quite impossible.

4.2 Steps for the Separation of Judiciary in Bangladesh: Pre-2007 Regime

In Bangladesh history, it is found that first attempt was taken in 1976 by a Law Committee of Justice Kamluddin Hossain who made a recommendation for the separation of the subordinate judiciary on the criminal side in three stages; in 1990 the separation of the judiciary was one of the commitment in the manifesto of three-party alliance but no steps were taken by the governments of 1991 & 1996 except spoiling their tenure; and it was Masdar Hossain, a district judge along with others 441 judicial officers brought a writ petition in 1995 to the HCD and of which consequence, the Appellate Division (hereinafter as AD) finally in 1999 gave necessary directions to the Government for the separation of the judiciary from the executive and legislature but 1996's government and

---

[218] Montesqueiu, *The Spirit of the Laws* 157 (Cambridge University Press, Cambridge, 1989), cited also in Sarkar Ali Akkas, Independence and Accountability of Judiciary-A Critical Review 17 (Center for Rights and Governance, Dhaka-1000, 2004).

[219] W Paley, "Moral and Political Philosophy" 345 (1824) cited in SAM J Ervin, 'Separation of Power: Judicial Independence' (1970) 35 Law and Contemporary Problems 108-127, available at: https://scholarship.law.duke.edu/cgi/viewcontent.cgi?referer=https://www.google.com/&httpsredir=1&article=3279&context=lcp (Last visited on May 27, 2018).

2001's government also excused many times and dissipated their tenure.[220] Finally, it was 1st November, 2007 the separation of judiciary was formally possible to be established by the then caretaker government with a view to fulfilling the mandatory directions of the *Masdar Hossain* judgment which is popularly known as separation of power case.

In Masdar *Hossain* case the petitioners claimed inter alia: i. inclusion of judicial service in the name of BCS (Judicial) under the Bangladesh Civil Services (Re-organization) Order, 1980 is ultra vires the Constitution; ii. Chapter II of Part VI of the constitution has already separated lower judiciary from executive where necessary amendments of article 115 may be required for full separation; iii. judges of the subordinate courts being presiding officers cannot be subject to the jurisdiction of administrative tribunal of the executive. The court gave landmark judgment in 1997 declaring 12 historical directions with a view to giving implementation of separation of judiciary from the executive. The AD of the SCB reversed the decision of the HCD upholding the 12 directions of the HCD in 1999 in a reply to the appeal of the government. This landmark decision is popularly called as *Masdar Hossain* Case where:

> 'The Appellate Division directed the Government to implement its 12 point directives, including for formation of separate Judicial Service Commission (JSC) to serve the appointment, promotion and transfer of members of the judiciary in consultation with the SC. A further 12-point directive called for a separate Judicial Service Pay Commission, amendment of the criminal procedure and the new rules for the selection and discipline of members of the Judiciary.'[221]

In the above mentioned case, the AD of the SCB declared and directed the government to implement the 12 directions where they are as under:

I. The judicial service is a service of the Republic within the meaning of Article 152(1) of the Constitution, but it is a functionally and structurally distinct and separate service from the executive and administrative services of the Republic.[222]

[220] Tania Lipi, 'Separation of Judiciary from the executive: an Evaluation and Analysis', available at: https://www.researchgate.net/.../238114298_Separation_of_Judiciary_and_Judicial_In... (Last visited on June 23, 2018).

[221] See Bangladesh Supreme Court Bar Association: Masdar Hossain Case available at: www.bangladeshsupremecourtbar.com/Masdar_Hossain_Case.php (Last visited on July 23, 2018).

[222] *Secretary, Ministry of Finance* v. *Md. Masdar Hossain and others* (1999) 52 DLR AD 82, para 76(1).

II. The word "appointment" in Article 115 means that it is the President who under Article 115 can create and establish a judicial service and also a magistracy exercising judicial functions, make recruitment rules and all pre appointment rules etc. but Article 115 does not contain any rulemaking authority with regard to other terms and conditions of service and that Article 133 and Article 136 of the constitution and the Services (Reorganization and Conditions) Act, 1975 have no application to the above matters in respect of judicial functions.[223]

III. The creation of BCS (Judicial) Cadre along with other BCS executive and administrative cadres by Bangladesh Civil Service (Re-organisation) Order 1980 with amendment of 1986 is ultra vires the Constitution, whereas Bangladesh Civil Service Recruitment Rules, 1981 are applicable to the judicial service.[224]

IV. The nomenclature of the judicial service shall follow the language of the Constitution and shall be designated as the Judicial Service of Bangladesh or Bangladesh Judicial Service. A Judicial Services Commission shall be established forthwith with majority of members from the Senior Judiciary of the Supreme Court and the subordinate courts for recruitment to the Judicial service on merit with the objective of achieving equality between men and women in the recruitment.[225]

V. Under Article 133 law or rules relating to posting promotion, grant of leave, discipline (except suspension and removal), pay, allowances, pension (as a matter of right not favour) and other terms and conditions of service, consistent with Articles 116 and 1 16A shall be enacted separately for the judicial service.[226]

VI. It is also directed to establish a separate Judicial Pay Commission forthwith as a part of the Rules to be framed under Article 115 to review the pay, allowances and other privileges of the judicial service. The pay etc. of the judicial service shall follow the recommendations of the Commission.[227]

VII. It is declared that in exercising control and discipline of person's employer in the judicial service and magistrates exercising judicial functions under Article 116 the views and opinion of the SC shall have primacy over those of the Executive.[228]

---

[223] *Id.* para 76 (2).
[224] *Id.* para 76 (3).
[225] *Id.* para 76 (4).
[226] *Id.* para 76 (5).
[227] *Id.* para 76 (6).
[228] *Id.* para 76 (7).

VIII. The conditions of judicial independence in Article 116A, elaborated in the judgment, namely (1) security of tenure, (2) security of salary and other benefits and pension and (3) institution independence from the parliament and the Executive shall be secured in the law or rules made under Article 133 or in the executive orders having the force of Rules.[229]

IX. The executive Government shall not require the SCB as to seek their approval to incur any expenditure on any item from the funds allocated to the Supreme Court in the annual budgets.[230]

X. It is declared that the members of the judicial service are within the jurisdiction of the administrative tribunal.[231]

XI. For the separation of the subordinate judiciary from the executive parliament can amend the constitution if necessary to make the separation more meaningful, pronounced, effective and complete.[232]

XII. It is declared that until the Judicial Pay Commission gives its first recommendation the salary of Judges in the judicial service will continue to be governed by status quo ants.[233]

4.3 Steps for the Implementation of the Directions of *Masdar Hossain Case* and Post-2007 Regime

The separation of judiciary is a precondition for the independence of judiciary which is a basic feature of the Constitution. If the judiciary can perform independently, the citizens' rights can never be endangered from any quarters and the judiciary will be respected as protector of citizens' constitutional rights. But in order to implement the constitutional mandates regarding the separation of judiciary particularly the subordinate judiciary from the executive, the nation had to wait about 36 years from its independence.

It is also said earlier that the famous case *Masdar Hossain v Secretary, Ministry of Finance* plays a vital role for establishing the independence of judiciary in Bangladesh.[234] The case also reflects the separation of powers among the three

---

[229] *Id.* para 76 (8).
[230] *Id.* para 76 (9).
[231] *Id.* para 76 (10).
[232] *Id.* para 76 (11).
[233] *Id.* para 76 (12).
[234] M Rafiqul Islam, "Independence of Judiciary-The Masdar Case" *The Daily Star* (Dhaka, 10 March 2014) available at: https://www.thedailystar.net/independence-of-the-judiciary-the-masdar-case-14760 (Last visit on September 8, 2018).

organs of the government.[235] The theory of separation of powers was clearly reflected through the 12 directives in the judgment of *Masdar Hossain* case.

In order to meet the constitutional mandate under Article 22 of the Constitution and implement the directions of *Masder Hossain's Judgment*, then the caretaker government took necessary steps to execute the directives of the *Masdar* case and ensure separation of the judiciary enacting four sets of rules and finally the judiciary in paper was separated from the executive on 1st Nov. 2007:

i. Bangladesh Judicial Service Commission Rules, 2007
ii. Bangladesh Judicial Service Pay Commission Rules, 2007
iii. Bangladesh Judicial Service Commission (Constitution of service, appointment on the service and suspension, removal and dismissal from the service) Rules, 2007
iv. Bangladesh Judicial Service (posting, promotion, grant of leave, control discipline and other condition of service) Rules, 2007

Though then Mr. Fakruddin Admed's caretaker government passed four sets of rules to implement the directions of the judgment but all four sets are not currently operating in practice; only the Bangladesh Judicial Service Commission Rules, 2007 are actively working by which candidates are primarily selected by the Bangladesh Judicial Service Commission through preliminary examination, written examination and viva voce for appointing judges of subordinate judiciary.

Bangladesh Judicial Service Commission (hereinafter as the Commission) is composed of 11 (eleven) members who are appointed under section 3 of the Bangladesh judicial Service Commission Rule 2007, by the President in consultation with the Chief Justice of SCB.[236] The commission is constituted with a judge of the AD as its chairman, two judges of the HCD, Attorney General, one member of the Law Commission, the Secretary, Ministry of Establishment, the Secretary, Ministry of Finance, the Secretary, Ministry of Law, and Justice, one of the Deans of the Faculty of Law of Dhaka University, Rajshahi University or Chittagong University, Registrar, Bangladesh Supreme Court and the district judge of Dhaka as members of the Commission. In addition to its regular responsibilities of selection of candidates for the appointment, the Commission is also responsible to give legal advice on any

[235] The World Bank, 'Legal and Judicial Capacity Building Project, Finance and Private Sector Department: South Asia Region' available at: http://documents.worldbank.org/curated/en/223531468007223731/pdf/ICR120001Public0Disclosed0July0121.pdf (Last visit on September 8, 2018).
[236] Bangladesh Judicial Service Commission Rule 2007, s3.

legal question regarding such appointment or duties of the Commission; the Commission have to perform the duties imposed upon it by the any other rules made under article 115 or 133 of the Constitution of Bangladesh[237] ; and the Commission has to submit annual reports of its annual activities to the President within 31st March of each year.[238] It has also power to enact any rules, which is not inconsistence with the BJSC Rules 2007, by official gazette notification in consultation with the President.[239]

It is apt to state that the appointment, posting, removal system of judges of the subordinate judiciary are not being fulfilled in pursuance of Bangladesh Judicial Service Commission [Constitution of service, appointment on the service and suspension, removal and dismissal from the service] Rules, 2007 and Bangladesh Judicial Service [posting, promotion, grant of leave, control discipline and other condition of service] Rules, 2007 consecutively. Rather the removal, promotion, posting and transfer of the judges of subordinate courts are preceded by the executive through the ministry of law and justice in consultation with the SCB which is deemed as main bar to establish true separation of judiciary.[240] Recently, Judicial Service Disciplinary Rules, 2017 have been passed but they have also some loopholes which are contradictory with the doctrine of separation of power discussed in the barriers section of the paper. On the other hand, the judges of the Supreme Court are also appointed by the executive on political consideration in consultation with the Supreme Court for which there is no detailed written rules in spite of directions[241] being issued from the SC upon the matter.

---

[237] *Id.* s. 5(3)
[238] *Id.* s. 7
[239] *Id.* s. 8
[240] Md. Milan Hossain, "Effective Judiciary and Citizens' Rights- A study: Bangladesh Perspective" 3(1), *AJLEG* (2017) available at: www.ajleg.net.au/index.php/AJLEG/article/view/28 (Last visited on August 28, 2018).
[241] In the case of *Idrisur Rahman* v. *Bangladesh* (2009) 61 DLR 523 the Supreme court gave twelve directions but they have not seen the light of implication:
(i) The proposal and process for the appointment of judges in both branches of the Supreme Court should emanate from the Chief Justice of Bangladesh.
(ii) The opinion of the Chief Justice in case of the appointment of judges in the higher judiciary is entitled to have the primacy.
(iii) The Chief Justice shall consult with two most senior judges of both, AD & HCD to form his opinion in case of appointment of judges to the High Court Division and with three most senior judges of Appellate Division for the appointment of judges in the AD.
(iv) The President or the government shall not have right to initiate for the appointment of judges in the Supreme Court of Bangladesh bypassing the Chief Justice but shall have right to suggest the name of judges.
(v) The reasons of non-appointment of judges recommended shall be disclosed and communicated to the Chief Justice for his opinion. And if he gets nothing by consulting such judges, he shall again recommend and the President must adhere such recommendation.
(vi) The President shall as a rule accept the recommendation of the Chief Justice for appointment of judges. If the recommendation of the Chief Justice could not be accepted by the President, it cannot be directly rejected

It is apposite to mention here that the traditional judgment reflects the judicial independence of Bangladesh where the Justice Latifur Rahman draws the reference of article 94 (4) of the Constitution which mandates *"Subject to the provisions of this constitution the chief justice and other judges shall be independent in the exercise of their judicial function"*. He also comments *"An independent judiciary is the conscience - keeper of the State."*[242] The leading case also mostly emphasizes upon the article 115, 116, 116A, 152 (1), 133, 136, 109, 117 which are directly and indirectly related to independence of judiciary. In this perspective, the court declared that article 94(4) and 116A of the Constitution as one of the basic pillars of the constitution and cannot be demolished, whittled down, curtailed or diminished in any manner.[243] The said case plays significant role in making rules for appointment of judges of Subordinate Judiciary by the Judicial Service Commission under Bangladesh Judicial Service Commission Rules, 2007. Actually, the fact is that the Judicial Service Commission can only make selection and recommendation of suitable candidates for appointing judges of Subordinate Judiciary where the executive exclusively exercises the power of appointment to the service and suspension, removal and dismissal from the service in pursuance of Article 115 of the Constitution.

From the study upon the directives of *Masdar Hossain* Judgment, it is revealed that first four directions, viz., Direction No.1: Judicial Service –distinct and separate service from the executive and administrative service; Direction No.2: Creating and Establishing Judicial Service including judicial magistracy; Direction No.3: Creation of BCS (Judicial) Cadre along with other BCS executive and administrative cadre Ultra Vires the Constitution and Direction

---

and new judges cannot be appointed on the government choice rather the recommendation shall send back to the Chief Justice for reconsideration of it.

(vii) After reconsideration if the Chief Justice may withdraw the recommendation but if he again recommends consult with the aforesaid senior most judges of the Appellate Division for appointment, the government shall be obliged to complete the process of appointment.

(viii) If the recommendation of the Chief Justice for appointment or non-appointment of an additional judge as judge under Article 95 of the constitution is disregarded by the Executive, violates the Constitution.

(ix) If the recommendation of chief justice is refused by the executive, the reason is to be recorded and is to send back for reconsideration on the materials and information conveyed.

(x) After such reconsideration if he again recommends for the appointment or non-appointment, the executive shall accept it without raising any question.

(xi) After successful completion of the period under Article 98, an additional judge shall be entitled to legitimate expectation to be appointed as permanent judge under Article 95.

(xii) Non-appointment of petitioners under the circumstances as stated under Article 95 violates the constitution and conventions and is accordingly declared to be arbitrary, malafide, without any lawful authority and as such, of no legal effect.

[242] *Secretary, Ministry of Finance* v. *Md. Masdar Hossain and others* (1999) 52 DLR AD 82, para 76(4).

[243] *Id.* para 57.

No.4: Establishment of Judicial Service Commission [244], Direction No. 6 (Establishment of Separate Judicial Pay Commission[245]) and Direction No. 10 are being merely implemented but rest of the directives of the case are yet to implement or still inactive. Because, in case of Direction No. 5 (pay, allowance, pension, terms and condition), Direction No. 7 (priority of Supreme Court over executive), and Direction No. 8 (security of tenure, salary and institutional independence), no effective actions are taken to implement them for the purpose of ensuring separation of judiciary and independence of judiciary.

In addition, in the while after separation some matters have been raised creating restraint in implementing true separation of the judiciary according to *Masdar Hossain's* Judgment directions, which cannot be ignored and therefore, they are analyzed here as under:

Contrary Provisions of the Constitution

Article 116A of the Constitution provides that all persons employed in the judicial service and even all magistrates[246] shall be independent in the exercise of their judicial functions. Again, Article 109 of the Constitution states that the SC shall have superintendence and control over all courts and subordinate to it. But the current Articles 115[247] and 116[248] of the Constitution have created a real

---

[244] Judicial Service Commission (hereinafter as JSC) after its constitution in 2007 under the JSC Rules, 2007 recommended names of 165 persons for appointment as assistant judges after their selection on the basis of oral and written examination held earlier by the Public Service Commission (PSC). In 2008, the Commission also arranged and conducted examination for selecting persons for appointment as assistant judges, and on its recommendation about 400 candidates have been appointed as assistant judges. (See Judicial Service Commission – Banglapedia, available at: en.banglapedia. org/index.php?title=Judicial_Service_Com (Last visited on 25 November 2018). Currently the commission is conducting 12th BJSC Assistant Judge Recruitment Exam for selecting candidates for appointing judges in subordinate judiciary (See 12th BJSC Assistant Judge Recruitment Exam Circular 2018 ... available at: https://www.bdresultjob.com/2018/03/BJSC.html (Last visited on 25 June 2018).

[245] The Judicial Service Pay Commission was established under Judicial Service Pay Commission Rules, 2007 that came into force after a directive by the Supreme Court on December 2, 1999 to separate lower judiciary from the executive branch. In 2015, the Commission recommended the highest basic pay of TK. 84,000 for a senior district judge and the lowest of TK. 35,000 for assistant judge. The Commission also urged for retaining the existing 30% judicial allowance the judicial officers have been enjoying since 2012.

See New Age – Judicial pay commission recommends pay hike for district ... available at: *archive.newagebd.net/.../judicial-pay-commission-recommends-pay-hike-for-district-l...* (Last visited on August 28, 2018).

[246] Judicial Magistrates; after 2007 magistrates are classified into two types in the Code of Criminal Procedure, 1908, namely:- (a) Judicial Magistrate; and (b) Executive Magistrate whereas Judicial Magistrate is of four types: (a) Chief Metropolitan Magistrate in Metropolitan Area and Chief judicial Magistrate to other areas; (b) Magistrate of the first class, who shall in Metropolitan area, be known as Metropolitan Magistrate; (c) Magistrate of the second class; and(d) Magistrate of the third class (Section 6)

[247] Current Article 115 was substituted by section 19 of the Constitution (Fourth Amendment) Act, 1975 (Act No. II of 1975)

[248] Article 116 was substituted for the former article 116 by section 32 of the Constitution (Fifteenth Amendment) Act, 2011); the Constitution (Fifteenth Amendment) Act, 2011 was the most debatable one in the post democratic era from 1990's public upsurge against autocracy; such amendment was introduced to the constitution by the two third majority of the total members of the Parliament with a view to repealing the

bar to a meaningful and effective separation and independence of the Judiciary. These two articles have empowered the President to make appointments of judges and judicial magistrates of the subordinate judiciary and to deal posting, promotion, discipline of judicial officers in consultation with the SC. In fact, under these two articles, the Executive can control and interfere over the lower judiciary regarding posting, promotion, discipline of judicial officers despite the judiciary being separated from the executive in paper as the President has limitation; in the exercise of all his functions he has to act according to the directions of the Chief Executive or Prime Minister as per view of Article 48(3)[249] which means the President can exercise all his functions at the desire of the Prime Minister of the Executive Head. Under these circumstances, the provisions of Articles 109, 115 and 116 have created 'dual rule[250]' in the Judiciary which sometimes makes slow the file of appointment, transfer, posting and promotion of the judges of lower courts at the district level. Under this contrary constitutional provisions which give a space to the Executive to interfere to the judiciary and due to reality, people believe that judges who issue orders or decisions against the interest of the government are transferred from their current job station (place of business) to inconvenient working stations;[251]in consequence, judges may give orders or judgments in favour of the government which is not helpful anyway to establish individual independence or institutional independence of the judiciary.

Despite the separation of lower judiciary from the executive, the posting, promotion, discipline of judicial officers are still interfered by the Executive due to the constitutional existing provisions. Therefore, effective separation and real independence either institutionally or individually are not possible. But there were no such provisions in the original Constitution of 1972. The Article 116 of the Constitution, 1972, empowered the SC to control over the lower judiciary in case of postings, promotions, grant of leave and discipline. As per Article 115 of the Constitution 1972, district judges would be appointed by the President on the

---

caretaker government from the constitution but along with this, many changes were introduced including the power to interfere with the lower judiciary under article 116 of the constitution which frustrated many (see Sanjida Yeasmin and Falgni Sutradhar, '*The 15th amendment of the consittituion and the confrontational politics*' available at: https://www.academia.edu/29363795/The_15th_amendment_of_the_constitution_and_the_confrontational_politics, (accessed on January 5 2020).

[249] As per article 48(3) it provides that "In the exercise of all his functions, save only that of appointing the Prime Minister pursuant to clause (3) of article 56 and the Chief Justice pursuant to clause (1) of article 95, the President shall act in accordance with the advice of the Prime Minister".

[250] The terms 'dual rule' means the control of the executive and the Supreme Court over the lower judiciary regarding posting, promotion, discipline of judicial officers as per present provisions of the constitution under articles 109, 115, 116.

[251] Mizanur Rahman Khan, "An Interview with Mr. Anisul Haque, Honable Minister, Law & Justice, Govt. of Republic of Bangladesh" *The Daily Prothom Alo* (Dhaka, 12 July, 2015) 10.

Supreme Court's recommendation. Under this situation, in order to ensure true separation, the Legislature should restore the original articles 115 and 116 in in place of current ones.

Tenure and Removal of Judges: State of Job Security

Article 94(4) of the Constitution provides that the Chief Justice and the other judges of the SC shall be independent in the exercise of their judicial functions. The security of tenure of judges, their promotion, posting and transfer are the core characteristics of the independence of the judiciary also admitted as essential element for the independence of the judiciary in the *Masdar Hossain Judgment*. In the judgment of the 16th Amendment case[252] Dr. Kamal Hossain also opined the security of the judges as one of the essential conditions for ensuring effective independence of the judiciary; the same view was also reflected in the case of *Walter Valente* v *Majesty The Queen and another*, (1985) 2 R.C.S. 673 and S.P Gupta and others v President of India and others, 19823 AIR (SC) 149 cited in the same judgment of the 16th Amendment case.[253] As per Article 96(1) a judge of the Supreme court shall hold office until he attains the age of 67 years; he/she cannot hold the office for life time; he/she may be removed from his/her office due to physical or mental incapacity, gross misconduct or moral turpitude for which if the Supreme Judicial Council[254] makes recommendation to the President. But such power of the Council has been taken away by the 16th Amendment of the Constitution and vested upon into the hands of the parliament members[255]; Under these circumstances, Article 96 of the Constitution containing the provisions for removal of the judges of the Supreme Court by the recommendation of the Supreme Judicial Council[256] is held in the 16th Amendment Case[257] as an integral part of the independence of the Judiciary as incorporated in the Constitution which is not amendable due to

---

[252] Writ petition no. 9989 of 2014, available at: https://www.supremecourt.gov.bd/resources/documents/783957_WP9989of2014.pdf (Last visited on September 9, 2018).

[253] See the Judgment of the HCD upon the 16th Amendment case, 41, available at: http://www.supremecourt.gov.bd/resources/documents/783957_WP9989of2014.pdf (Last visited on September 9, 2018).

[254] Supreme Judicial Council consists of 3 members from the judges of the Supreme Court incorporated in the constitution of which one member is chief justice and next two senior judges of the Supreme Court.

[255] As per 16th Amendment of the constitution, Article 96(2) provides "A Judge shall not be removed from his office except by an order of the President passed pursuant to a resolution of Parliament supported by a majority of not less than two-thirds of the total number of members of Parliament, on the ground of proved misbehaviour or incapacity."

[256] A council of three members inserted in the Constitution under Article 96 by the 5th Amendment of the Constitution; of which one member is chief justice and next two senior judges of the Supreme Court where Article 96(2) of the Constitution provides that a Judge of the Supreme Court shall not be removed from his office except a report submitted to the President by the Supreme Judicial Council on basis of an inquiry proceeded by it due to the allegation of physical or mental incapacity, gross misconduct or moral turpitude regarding a judge of the Supreme Court.

[257] Civil Appeal No.06 of 2017, available at: http://www.supremecourt.gov.bd/resources/documents/1082040_C.A.6of17.pdf (Last visited on August 31, 2018).

the provision of Article 7B inserted by the 15th Amendment of the Constitution. But the independence of judiciary has been affected by the 16th Amendment of the Constitution[258] as it empowers the Parliament to remove the judges of the Supreme Court of Bangladesh which is direct interference of Legislature with the Judiciary and contravention of constitutional provisions. Therefore, the independence of judiciary has been affected and subsequently such amendment was declared as void (illegal) in recent judicial pronouncements[259] of the HCD and AD in the 16th Amendment Case; now this case is pending before the AD for review; due to harsh observations[260] in the judgment the relation among the judiciary, executive, and legislature emerged as the worst in the history of the country and there was high tension among the judiciary and the government and consequence of which, the former chief justice S K Sinha was compelled to resign; justice Wahab Miah had to act as chief justice- in- charge and later he also resigned due to appointing another justice as chief justice of the SCB in transgression of the seniority rule.[261]Under these circumstances, it is harsh and challenging for the judges to exercise their judicial functions independently.

Mobile Court[262]

The trial by mobile courts held by the executive magistrates raise questions among the citizens as regards the independence of judiciary in the country and

[258] By the 16th Amendment of the Constitution the provision of the Supreme Judicial Council was repealed and the Parliament (legislature) has been empowered to remove the judges of the Supreme Court where new provision is as: "A Judge shall not be removed from his office except by an order of the President passed pursuant to a resolution of Parliament supported by a majority of not less than two-thirds of the total number of members of Parliament, on the ground of proved misbehaviour or incapacity."

[259] Writ petition no. 9989 of 2014, available at: https://www.supremecourt.gov.bd/resources/documents/783957_WP9989of2014.pdf (Last visited on September 9, 2018) & As per 16th Amendment of the constitution, Article 96(2) provides "A Judge shall not be removed from his office except by an order of the President passed pursuant to a resolution of Parliament supported by a majority of not less than two-thirds of the total number of members of Parliament, on the ground of proved misbehaviour or incapacity."

[260] The Appellate Division of the Supreme Court of Bangladesh made several observations: (i) Executive becomes arrogant, uncontrolled; (ii) Having no check and balances; (iii) Parliament is dysfunctional; (iv) Corruption is rampant; (v) Human rights are at stake; (vi) Mismanagement in the administration is acute; (vii) Politics as an institution is completely destroyed; (viii) Instead of strengthening the Judiciary, the executive is now trying to cripple it and if it happens, there could be disastrous consequences and so on.

[261] Principle of seniority is deemed as an important factor in the case of appointment of judges from High Court Division to the Appellate Division; such principle by practice has created but there no recognition in the Constitution or in the Statutes; See Sarkar Ali Akkas, Independence and Accountability of Judiciary-A Critical Review (Center for Rights and Goverance, Dhaka-1000, 2004)17.

[262] Mobile Courts are special courts moving one place to another held by the executive for summary trial of particular offences with a view to maintaining law and order of the country and preventing the commission of the particular offences (See The Mobile Court Act, 2009, available at: http://www.gaibandha.gov.bd/sites/default/files/files/www.gaibandha.gov.bd/page/6f577055_18fd_11e7_9461_286ed488c766/Mobile%20court%20act%202009.pdf, and see also GD Hosen and SR Ferdous, '*The Role of Mobile Court in the Enforcement of Laws in Bangladesh*' NUJL (2010) 1, available at: file:///C:/Users/HP/Downloads/18527-Article%20Text-66678-1-10-20140407.pdf, (Last visited on January 5, 2020).

such trials often infringe rights of citizens[263]; it is a direct interference by the executive with the functions of judiciary, which is also conflicting to citizen's right regarding fair trial by the open court enshrined in Article 35 of the Constitution; conviction by mobile court on the basis of testimony of witnesses and circumstantial evidence without giving any opportunity to accused to consult with a lawyer and without his confession is clear violation of citizens' fundamental rights enshrined in the Constitution which is also contrary to the separation of judiciary and to the Judgment of *Masdar Hossain Case.*[264] "Trial of mobile court by executive magistrate creates double judiciary system in the country as they are not under the control and supervision of the Supreme court of Bangladesh as it having upon other subordinate courts; why it is running in this way"- asked by the then chief Justice Surendra Kumar Sinha in the seminar held at Dhaka University (DU) Senate Bhavan.[265] Even this peculiar trial by Executive is not found and existent in India and Pakistan.[266] In the case of the trial of mobile courts by executive magistrates, "check and balance should be ensured while executive magistrates try through mobile courts, they should come under the supervision of the SC" –admitted by the present law minister-Mr Anisul Haque in an interview taken by Prothom Alo[267]. Even the HCD declared the mobile court as unconstitutional in the year (2017) in the judgment of the Mobile Court Case, 2017.[268] The court also opined that empowering the executive magistrates with judicial powers as "a frontal attack on the independence of the judiciary and overstepping of the theory of the separation of powers". After such judgment from the HCD, the govt. made three appeal petitions to the AD against the verdict and got permission to run the activities of such courts until the disposal of three leave to appeal petitions[269].

---

[263] Shakhawat Liton and Ahuthosh Sarkar, "Mobile Court Trials often violate rights'' *The Daily Star* (Dhaka, 6 August 2015)1.

[264] Staff Correspondent, 'Conviction may be drawn without confession' *The Prothom Alo (*Dhaka, 23 June 2015) 20.

[265] Staff Correspondent, "Fair Justice Not Possible for Murder of Tanu under old laws" *The Prothom Alo(*Dhaka, 3 April, 2016) 1, 4.

[266] Writ petition no. 9989 of 2014, available at: https://www.supremecourt.gov.bd/resources/documents /783957_WP9989of2014.pdf (Last visited on September 9, 2018).

[267] Mizanur Rahman Khan, "An Interview with Mr. Anisul Haque, Honable Minister, Law & Justice, Govt. of Republic of Bangladesh" *The Daily Prothom Alo* (Dhaka, 27 January 2016) 1,11

[268] Writ no. 8437 & 10482 of 2011, and 4879 of 2012, available at: www.supremecourt.gov.bd/resources/ documents/382548_WP8437of2011.pdf, (Last visited on June 25, 2018).

[269] Staff Correspondent, "Mobile Court can operate until disposal of petitions" *The Daily Star* (Dhaka, 10 January 2018) 1, available at: https://www.thedailystar.net/backpage/bangladesh-mobile-court-operation-can-operate-until-disposal-petitions-1517548 (Last visited on March 6, 2019).

Separate Secretariat for Judiciary

Despite the judiciary has been separated from the executive, no distinct or separate ministry or secretariat is yet to establish. The current 'ministry of law and justice' is working as secretariat for law and judiciary where the main tasks of 'the ministry of law and justice' are exercising as the administrative control, management and dealings with the sub-ordinate/attached departments or offices, namely, the sub-ordinate Judiciary, Administrative tribunals, various other special Courts and Tribunals, Department of Registration, Office of the Attorney-General, Judicial Administration Training Institute, Office of the Administrator General and official Trustee (AGOT), Judicial Service Commission Secretariat, Marriage Registration, Government Pleaders, Public Prosecutors, Notary Public, etc. More specifically the ministry gives advice to all ministers regarding the questions arising legal and constitutional matters; deals with other countries in judicial matters, takes steps for the administration of justice including appointing, posting, transfer, etc. of all judicial officers, take fees in courts and tribunals; judicial stamps, court-fees and stamp duties etc. appointing attorney general, deputy attorney general, assistant attorney general and assigning their functions etc.[270]

Due to the nature of the functions of 'the ministry of law and justice', there is often interference from the law ministry or government with the affairs and functions of the judiciary for which 'dual rule' is created in the judiciary which may make the necessary actions in slow in the case of appointment, transfer, promotion or posting of the judges of the lower judiciary which hinders the functions of the judiciary[271]. People believe that this ministry works for government more than to judiciary and interferes for the sake of the executive bodies or for the legislature. In several cases, the news come in daily newspapers regarding dubious role of this ministry: SC says President 'misinformed' on rules for the judges of lower court (subordinate courts) –this news came in The Daily Star, 13th Dec. 2016 where the SC asked the law ministry to issue a gazette notification on the rules determining the discipline and conduct of subordinate courts' judges. In a survey conducted by the researcher, 71.82% respondents among 30 judicial officers agreed on condition not disclosing their name for the sake of the job security that there should have a separate and independent secretariat for the judiciary for ensuring true

[270] See Government of the People's Republic of Bangladesh, Law and Justice Division, available at: http://old.lawjusticediv.gov.bd/static/about_us.php, (last visited on 10 January 2020).
[271] MN Huda, 'Independent Judiciary a must for democracy', The Daily Star (Dhaka, 27March2017), available at: https://www.thedailystar.net/opinion/straight-line/independent-judiciary-must-democracy-1381690, (last visited on on 12 January 2020).

independence of judiciary. Even the Supreme Court Bar Association (SCBA) demanded a separate secretariat in the light of the *Masdar Hossain* case verdict for the judiciary which will help to ensure judicial independence.[272] In reply to the SCBA demand's the law minister Mr. Anisul Haq remarked it as unrealistic as there is no separate secretariat for the judiciary for any democratic or undemocratic countries in the world.[273] But in an inquiry to this matters it is revealed that there is the ministry of justice headed by the Secretary of the State for justice in UK[274], or minister of justice in Canada[275] who is the minister of the Crown in the Canadian Cabinet, responsible for the Department of Justice, serves also as chief federal legal advisor and Attorney General of Canada. If here there is separate ministry for the judiciary rather than combined ministry (ministry of law and justice), it will work only for the judiciary; the consequence of which, the independence of the judiciary will be ensured; the judicial functions will run more smoothly and justice will be speedier.

Absence of Separate Investigation Cell and Independent Prosecution Service

In Bangladesh Subordinate Judiciary particularly judicial magistrate courts have no separate investigation cell. There are no judicial investigation officers under the supervision and control of the Judiciary and therefore, the judiciary has to depend on the police personnel who are under the control of State Ministry, maintaining law and order of the country, engaged in a myriad of issues showing a dillydally approach in casual manner in investigation. In many cases, they are alleged to be inefficient, negligent and biased in discharging their duties.[276] Even these police officers are not so skilled and experts for preparing reports and therefore, the accused get discharge due to weak investigation reports and therefore, citizens are deprived of justice. Besides, the police are so interested to

---

[272] 'SCAB demands separate secretariat for judiciary' *Dhaka Tribune* (Dhaka, 5 January 2018) available at: https://www.dhakatribune.com/bangladesh/court/2018/01/05/scba-demands-separate-secretariat-judiciary> (Last visited on September 10, 2018).

[273] 'SCAB demand of separate secretariat for judiciary unrealistic: Law Minister' *The Daily Star* (Dhaka, 7 January 2018) available at: https://www.thedailystar.net/politics/demand-separate-secretariat-judiciary-unrealistic-bangladesh-law-minister-supreme-court-bar-gazette-1516231 (Last visited on September 10, 2018).

[274] Ministry of Justice (United Kingdom), 2018, available at: https://www.gov.uk/government/organisations/ministry-of-justice (Last visited on September 11, 2018).

[275] Minister of Justice (Canada) 2018, available at: http://www.justice.gc.ca/eng/ (Last visited on September 11, 2018).

[276] Hussain MFB, 'An Appraisal of Criminal Investigation in Bangladesh' (2015) 60(2) Journal of Asiatic Society (Humanities) available at: www.asiaticsociety.org.bd/journal/H_December_2015/1%20H_885_D2015.pdf (Last visited on September 15, 2018).

arrest the criminals and so reluctant to present the witnesses before the courts, the consequence of which is very frustrating result in disposal of cases.[277]

Again, here there is no independent public prosecution service like many other countries of the world; public prosecutors are appointed here mostly on the basis of political consideration; ruling party appoints those lawyers who are loyal to them; therefore, inexperienced and unskilled lawyers are getting appointment who cannot insure justice due to their limitation; they are often also engaged in corruption [278] . But a prompt and quality investigation and independent prosecution service are required as a basis of a criminal case for ensuring quick and effective criminal justice. In India in 2012 separate investigation and prosecution cadre were proposed for speedy criminal trial system.[279] In Pakistan for the purpose of prosecution, separate police sub cadre is created where law graduates are being appointed to whom the judiciary has control and supervision.[280]In Bangladesh if such cadre is established, a speedy criminal trial system and effective separation of judiciary will be ensured. Under these circumstances, there is no alternative of separate investigation cell under the control of the judiciary and independent public prosecutor service.

Absence of Financial Independence

Financial independence is very essential for an effective separation and independence of the judiciary. According to Justice Browne –Wilkinson, the lack of financial support by the government is a threat to the independence of the judiciary. Justice Malcolm stated that 'the preparation of judicial estimates by anyone not acting under the direction of the judiciary and the exercise of control by the Government over the way in which the courts expend the funds granted to them necessarily poses a potential threat to judicial independence'.[281]

The financial independence for an effective independent judiciary and smooth judicial functions are also recognized by international instruments: Principle 7 of

[277] Surendra Kumar Sinha, "The Contribution of the Judiciary" *The Ittefaq* (Dhaka, 25 December, 2016)8 available at: http://epaper.ittefaq.com.bd/?archiev=yes&arch_date=25-12-2016# (Last visited on 29 August 2018).

[278] MSI Tipu and AI SHaon, "Why we need an independent public prosecution service" *DhakaTribune,* available at: https://www.dhakatribune.com/bangladesh/2017/07/06/need-independent-public-prosecution-service (Last visited on 10 January 2020).

[279] Press Information Bureau, Govt. of India, Separate Investigation and Prosecution Cadre Proposed for Speedy Criminal Justice, 2012, available at: http://pib.nic.in/newsite/PrintRelease.aspx?relid=80575(Last visited on September 15, 2018).

[280] Tofail Ahmed, "*Britto O Brithantho: Bikendrikaran, Shathania Shasan, Rajnithi O Unnayan Bhabna*" 184 (in Bangla) (Dhaka, Agamee Prokashani, 2011).

[281] Citied in a consultation paper on the Financial Autonomy of Indian Judiciary (Chap:V, 5.19) available at: http://legalaffairs.gov.in/sites/default/files/Financial%20Autonomy%20of%20the%20Indian%20Judiciary.pdf (Last visited on February 2, 2019).

UN Basic Principles on the Independence of the Judiciary provides that it is the duty of a State to provide adequate resources to the judiciary to ensure its proper judicial functions[282]; again Article 34 of the Draft Universal Declaration on the Independence of Justice states that for ensuring the independence of the judiciary the budget for the judiciary shall be prepared by the proper authority in collaboration with the judiciary regarding needs and requirements of the judiciary.[283] Even in the judgment of the *Masdar Hossain* case, it is opined that the higher judiciary should get financial independence for effective and meaningful discharging of judicial functions especially for constitutional functions.[284] Officially the judiciary is separated from the Executive in 2007 but the judiciary has no financial independence still today due to having no self-fund of it; the revenue coming from the court fees are deposited to the Govt. fund; the Judiciary has to depend on the government and the govt. what amount allocates each year for the judiciary is very inadequate; actually judiciary gets less than 1% of the total budget of the country.[285] In the financial year-2016, only 112 cores were allocated for judiciary which was very poor for infrastructure development of the judiciary but the govt. earns more from court fees. Even the then chief justice also urged for financial independence of the judiciary.[286] The current state of financial independence and budget for the judiciary are not improving as in the financial year (2019-2020) only 195 cores are being proposed for the Supreme Court of Bangladesh where for whole judiciary it is 1650 cores which is only .352 percent of total budget in spite of being one of the three organs of the State whereas the allocated budget for BTV or Fishing Department is far more.[287] Under this poor budget it is quite impossible to work as an effective independent organ to upgrade the rule of law in the country.

Judicial Service Conduct & Discipline Rules 2017

One of the directions of *Masdar Hossain Case* was to make separate and different rules on the discipline and conduct of judges of the subordinate courts but upto 2017, no gazette notification is issued. On several occasions, the SC expressed dissatisfaction with the government for not finalizing the Conduct Rules. On the 7th May, 2016 the Law Ministry made a proposed rules on the

---

[282] UN Basic Principles on the Independence of the Judiciary, 1985, available at: https://www.un.org/ruleoflaw /blog/document/basic-principles-on-the-independence-of-the-judiciary/ (Last visited on September 11, 2018).
[283] Draft Universal Declaration on the Independence of Justice, 1989, available at: https://www.cristidan ilet.ro/docs/Shingvi%20Declaration.pdf (Last visited September 11, 2018).
[284] *Secretary, Ministry of Finance v. Masdar Hossain and others,* 52 DLR (AD) 82, Para. 89.
[285] Shadin Malik, "*Hatee Gora Gelo Tol*" (Horse Elephant Gone to Under) *The Prothom Alo*, (Dhaka, 29 June 2016) 11.
[286] *Id.*
[287] Eqramul Haque Shamim, Backlog in the Judiciary V Disposal, *Lawyers Club Bangladesh.com.* (2019, June 20). Retrieved from http://lawyersclubbangladesh.com/2019/06/20/ (accessed on 12 January, 2020).

discipline and conduct of the judges for lower courts and sent it to the SC for opinion which was rejected on 28th August, 2016 at the hearing of *Masdar Hossain Case* by the Supreme Court due to similar of the Govt. Employees (Discipline & Appeal) Rules, 1985 which was totally contrary to the judgment of *Masdar Hossain* Case. Under these circumstances, the SC showed its dissatisfaction and gave a draft copy on the Rules to the 'Ministry of Law and Justice' to publish it by gazette notification. [288] But an embarrassing and surprising matter arose while law ministry issued a notification on the 11th Dec. 2016 stating that the President decided not to issue a separate gazette notification on the conduct rules.[289] Finally, after resignation of the former chief justice, SK Sinha, the govt. issued and published the gazette notification for the Judicial Service Conduct & Discipline Rules 2017 but in the Rules old things are found as new ones regarding the final authority relating to the suspension, removal or temporary suspension of judges of the subordinate courts; here in the case of the suspension, removal or temporary suspension of the judges of the subordinate courts, the President (who has to act according to the advice of the head of the executive or prime minister[290]) is referred to as final authority in the name of appropriate authority and the higher authority refers to the SC and district judge.[291] Therefore, it is evident that ultimate power is still in the hand of the executive by the name of the President as titular head of the state. As a result, the spirit of original Constitution (1972's Constitution) and the directions of the *Masdar Case* regarding the separation and independence of the judiciary are not truly reflected and implemented. Interestingly, again, the shadow of the 'dual rule' is also reflected under the Rules, 2017 through the name of appropriate authority regarding removal, suspension, or temporary suspension of judges of the lower courts. More interestingly, it is seen that the SC has welcomed such Rules 2017 without raising any question; they have accepted it. Under these circumstances, a column in the Daily Star[292] titled "A collective failure" had come out on 9th January, 2018 explaining the reasons behind the responsibility for not establishing effective separation and independence of the judiciary after 19 years being passed from the *Masdar Hossain* Judgment. However, finally, it can be said that such separate rules for the conduct of judges of the lower judiciary are the old things in the new bottle by the executive where

[288] Staff Correspondent, "Judiciary is independent but preserved in a box locked" –said CJ to the Attorney General' *The Ittefaq* (Dhaka, 7November, 2016) 1, 19.
[289] Staff Correspondent, 'Rules For Lower Court Judges' *The Daily Star* (Dhaka, 13 December 2016)1, 10.
[290] See the Article 48(3) of the Constitution, available at: http://bdlaws.minlaw.gov.bd/act-details-367.html, (Accessed 12 January, 2020).
[291] Judicial Service Conduct & Discipline Rules 2017, rr. 2, 11, 15
[292] Shakhawat Liton, "A Collective Failure" *The Daily Star* (Dhaka, 9th January 2018) available at: https://www.thedailystar.net/frontpage/collective-failure-1517050 (Last visited on August 13, 2018).

the executive claims a progressive step though the effective separation of judiciary is still today absent in practice.

Conclusion

In Bangladesh 'the role of each organ of the State is clearly defined and deliberately and carefully kept separate under the constitution to maintain its harmony and integrity and to maximize the effectiveness of the functionality of the organs of the State in their respective spheres'.[293] But the Judiciary is formally separated in 2007 by the separation of the judicial magistrate courts from the Executive accompanying some drawbacks where the appointment of judicial officers of the lower judiciary, their posting, promotion and removal still today depend on the President under current Articles 115 & 116 of the Constitution and under the Rules 2017; there is no separate secretariat for judiciary and detailed specified rules for the appointment of judges for higher judiciary.

In this paper in response to inquiry it is also revealed that some directions of the *Masdar Hossain* case have been fulfilled and few will not see the light of implementation (see post-2007 regime section). It is also found that trial by mobile court held by the Executive is creating double judiciary in the country which is not under the supervision and control of the SC for which the separation of the judiciary is again at stake; in addition to this, the dilemma of the judgment of the 16th amendment case and subsequent consequences (implied confinement of former chief justice, then resignation, chief justice in-charge, infringement of the seniority principle and resignation of the aggrieved judges) have raised questions among the people of the country regarding the separation of the judiciary and therefore, the independence of the judiciary has fallen into huge challenge.

Apart from these, the financial independence of judiciary is yet to be established; due to lack of separate investigation cell under the Judiciary and absence of independent prosecution service, an effective separation is not established; the people are depriving of speedy criminal trial system; as a result, they are losing their confidence upon the judiciary. With a view to implementing the directions of the *Masdar Hossain* Judgment, separate code of conduct or discipline rules for the judges of the lower judiciary was passed in 2017 which was deemed as old things in a new bottle as the ultimate authority being vested in the hand of

---

[293] See the Judgment of the HCD upon the 16th Amendment case, 41, available at: http://www.supremecourt.gov.bd/resources/documents/783957_WP9989of2014.pdf (Last visited on September 9, 2018).

the executive via the president regarding the removal of judges of the lower judiciary against which the higher judiciary did not raise any questions which was deemed as collective failure of the judiciary, executive and legislature for not ensuring separation of the judiciary and independence of the judiciary.

In order to ensure the true separation of the judiciary, the 12 directives of the *Masdar Hossain* case need to be implemented and existing barriers in the judiciary identified in the paper are to be removed by the government so far as possible. In this regard, government positive-will should be raised through increasing awareness among the people by judicial authority, mass media and civil society. It is true that a government does not like the true separation of the powers of three organs of a state due to the excuses of the executive body. But, there is no alternative of separation of the judiciary from the executive and legislature as it is most important component to establish good governance and enforce citizens' rights. As, it is also opined by the High Court Division in the Judgment of the Mobile Court Case, 2017[294] that "if the independence of the Judiciary remains truly separate and distinct from the Legislature and the Executive, the people's power will never be endangered."[295]

[294] Staff Correspondent, "Mobile Court can operate until disposal of petitions" *The Daily Star* (Dhaka, 10 January 2018) 1, available at: https://www.thedailystar.net/backpage/bangladesh-mobile-court-operation-can-operate-until-disposal-petitions-1517548 (Last visited on March 6, 2019).
[295] The same views came in the case of *The State v. Chief Editor, Manabjamin*, [2005] 57 DLR (HCD) 359, the base of which was found in Montesquieu's book 'Spirit of Laws', Vol.-1, p. 181.

Chapter 5:

Judiciary and Rule of Law in the Post Separation Period –An Evaluation[296]

Introduction

As an important organ of the state, the ultimate responsibility of the judiciary is to enforce and upgrade the rule of law in the State. For doing this, the judiciary is empowered to dispose of disputed matters among the litigants (between individual and individual, individuals and government) brought before the courts without any discrimination in the open courts in accordance with law or by law; and the higher judiciary (the Supreme Court of Bangladesh) are also empowered by the Constitution under Article 102 to examine the actions of the executive, legislature or even the functions of the lower judiciary on the ground of ultra vires or arbitrary actions.

The Preamble of the Constitution urges the rule of law as one of the objectives (others are fundamental human rights and freedom, equality and justice) to be secured for all citizens. In *Anwar Hossain Chowdhury* case (popularly known as Eight Amendment Case) [1989 BLD (SPL) 1] it was observed that "it is the Judiciary which is entrusted with the task of keeping every organ of the State within the limits of the law and thereby making the rule of law meaningful and effective". And it is the Judiciary which upgrades the rule of law and ensures the protection of citizens' legal and constitutional rights even by issuing directions, recommendations and guidelines if there is vacuum in the law until a suitable law is enacted.

It is observed in *BLAST & Others v Bangladesh & Others* (2015) 1SCOB AD 2 that in order to achieve the rule of law the Constitution has assigned an onerous task upon the Judiciary and it is through the courts, the rule of law unfolds its contents where legal certainty will be ensured; each citizen will be treated as equal before the law. And an independent judiciary can establish the rule of law

[296] The author depends in conducting this chapter upon his PhD thesis titled 'Judiciary and Citizens Rights: Bangladesh Perspective (Not-Published) and the published journal paper titled 'The Role of Bangladesh Judiciary in Establishing and Promoting the Rule of Law in the Country: An Evaluation'. 6(5) International Journal of Law (IJL) p. 382-389.

by judicial review of administrative, legislative or even judiciary's actions (Dr. Kamal, 16th Amendment Case).

As the prime responsibility of the judiciary is to uphold the rule of law and if the judiciary can do it, the ruler will be prevented from abusing its powers which ensures the establishment of rule of law and justice to the affected citizens (the 16th Amendment case). It is also observed in the same judgment that unless the rule of law is established the citizens of a country will be deprived of the fruits of justice and also of citizens' rights. Because of the rule of law requires the protection of the fundamental rights of the citizens against the government.

It is mentioned earlier that the independence of the Judiciary is an essential element for rule of law but the notion of independence of the Judiciary is not limited to the concept that there will be no interference from the Legislature or the Executive as the Judiciary manned by the Judges are not independent, then how can say that the Judiciary is independent? Therefore, in order to establish rule of law and upgrade it, the Judiciary and its Judges must discharge their responsibilities without any pressure from the legislature or the executive or from any other pressure from any quarters of the society. Therefore, the judiciary must be separate and independent for discharging its onerous responsibility. Bangladesh Judiciary particularly judicial magistrate courts are formally separated on 1st Nov. 2007. After from this separation what role has the judiciary discharged with a view to enforcing and upgrading the rule of law in the country has been evaluated in this chapter.

5.1 Rule of Law

The rule of law has different meanings; firstly it means that everything must be done in accordance with law; secondly it means that the government should work within a fixed frame-work of rules and principles, for which transgression the judiciary can interfere to ensure citizens' rights either fundamental or non – fundamental; and thirdly it means that the disputes as to the legality of acts of government are to be decided by the judiciary without any pressure from the executive (61 DLR 523). A. V. Diecy's concept on rule of law has also three meanings from similar approach: (i) the supremacy of regular laws as opposed to the influence of arbitrary power by the persons in authority, (ii) equality before law where every citizen, whatever his rank or position is subject to ordinary laws and the jurisdiction of the courts and (iii) individual liberties legally protected not through any bill of rights but thorough the development of common law. It's true that A. V. Diecy's theory on rule of law were criticized by the critics from different angles but his emphasis on the subjection of every person to the ordinary law of the State, absence of arbitrary power and legal protection for certain basic human rights remains undisputed theme of the doctrine of rule of law (cited in 16th Amendment case). Davis in his book "Administrative Law" (1959) mentions seven principal meanings of the theory 'rule of law' which is presently more acceptable than Dicey's theory of rule of law: (i) law and order, (ii) fixed rules, (iii) elimination of discretion, (iv) due process of law or fairness, (v) natural law or observance of the principles of natural justice, (vi) preference for judges or ordinary courts of law to execute authorities and administrative tribunals, and (vii) judicial review of administrative actions (cited in 8 SCOB AD1). And these theories are guiding principles to address the role of the judiciary in upgrading the rule of law in the society. These principles are very settled and recognized in our constitution and court practices. As the citizens are entitled to enjoy his rights in accordance with law, under law and by law, where the judiciary or courts are bound to discharge its responsibility according to law, under law and by law for ensuring free and fair justice and upgrading the rule of law.

5.2 The Role of Judiciary

There are three organs of a State: (a) the Legislature, (b) the Executive and (c) the Judiciary where these three limbs of the state have a close connection to each other in maintaining rule of law particularly the judiciary has to play important role in ensuring rule of law. The judiciary of a country comprises all courts and tribunals which interpret law, settle legal disputes, enforce rights of citizens and impose penalty to the offenders and examine the functions of the executive, legislature and even subordinate judiciary and thus upgrade the rule of law in country. The Judiciary of Bangladesh can be drawn broadly by the Supreme Court (higher judiciary) and subordinate courts (lower judiciary). What was the role of judiciary in ensuring and upgrading the rule of law in the country after separation is a matter of research? For the purpose of the study, judicial magistrate courts, district civil courts from the subordinate judiciary & writ courts (Benches of HCD) from the higher judiciary are selected as targeted courts. By analyzing the performance of the concerned courts in the post separation period and comparing with the performances of pre-separation period, the role of judiciary can be determined in upholding the rule of law in the said period.

5.2.1 The Role of District Civil Courts

There are five kinds of civil courts in each district of the country: i) the court of District Judge, ii) the court of additional District Judge, iii) the court of Joint District Judge, iv) the court of Senior Assistant Judge and v) the court of Assistant Judge. These courts dispose of suits of civil nature. And it is the onerous obligation of civil courts to provide remedies to the victims on the basis of law and evidence produced by parties. In order to know what performance is shown by district civil courts in the period (2008-2016), it is required to compare between filing and disposing of suits in the mentioned courts in yearly basis:

Table No.5.1: Number of Filing & Disposal of Suits in the District Civil Courts during the Period (2008-2016)

Year	Filing New Suits	Disposal of Suits	Remarks
2008	1,65,339	1,10003	Disposal < Filing
2009	2,18,275	1,16,711	Disposal < Filing
2010	2,17,537	1,71,604	Disposal < Filing
2011	1,08,689	46,111	Disposal < Filing
2012	2,26,754	58,923	Disposal < Filing
2013	4,36,196	2,36,220	Disposal < Filing
2014	4,33,210	3,22,461	Disposal < Filing
2015	3,32,677	2,66,333	Disposal < Filing
2016	2,43,366	2,24,615	Disposal < Filing

Source: Annual Reports, 2008-2016, HCD, Supreme Court of Bangladesh

From the above table, one thing is very clear that the disposal rate is lesser than filing in this period particularly from the year-2008 to 2016. At the end of year-2007, there were 4, 56,604 suits pending for disposal (Annual Report, 2008, HCD, Supreme Court). And at the end of year-2016, pending suits stand as 12, 05,254(Annual Report, 2016, HCD, Supreme Court). Therefore, new pending suits stand in this period as 7,48,650 (Seven Lakh Forty-Eight Thousand Six Hundred Fifty) in the said period. The new pending cases in this period are almost thrice in comparing with pre-separation period (1972-2007).

Figure No.5.1: Trend of Filing and Disposal of Cases by District Civil Courts during the Period (2008-2016)

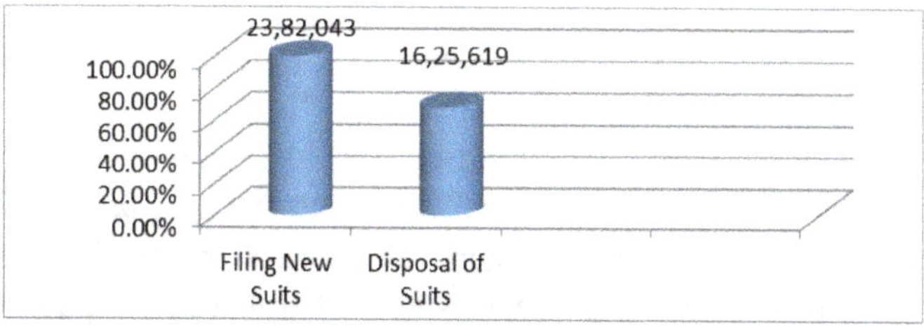

Source: Table 5.1

From the above data mentioned in Table No. 5.1 & Figure No. 5.1 it is evident that 68.24% of the total filing suits have been disposed of by the district civil courts in the period of (2008-2016) excluding backlog of cases of previous years (before 2008). The trend of filing, disposing of and pending of suits in the district civil courts can be exposed in the following figure:

Figure No.5.2: Trend of Filing, Disposal of and Pending of Suits by District Civil Courts during the Period (2008-2016)

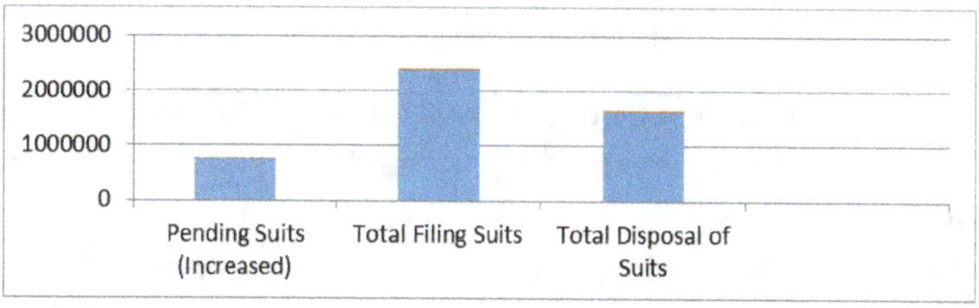

Source: Table No. 5.1

5.2.2 The Role of Judicial Magistrate Courts

Under the Code of Criminal Procedure, 1898 (hereinafter as CrPC) there shall be two classes of Criminal Courts in Bangladesh besides the Supreme Court and the Courts constituted under any law, namely:- (a) Courts of Sessions ; and(b) Courts of Magistrates; Magistrate court is of two types, namely:- (a) Judicial Magistrate; and (b) Executive Magistrate whereas Judicial Magistrate is of four types: (a) Chief Metropolitan Magistrate in Metropolitan Area and Chief judicial Magistrate to other areas; (b) Magistrate of the first class, who shall in Metropolitan area, be known as Metropolitan Magistrate; (c) Magistrate of the second class; and(d) Magistrate of the third class (CrPC, s. 6).

The Courts of Magistrates may pass sentences in the following ways: (a) Courts (of Metropolitan Magistrates and) of Magistrates of the first class: Imprisonment for a term not exceeding (five years) and fine not exceeding (ten thousand taka); (b) Courts of Magistrates of the second class: Imprisonment for a term not exceeding (three years),and Fine not exceeding (five thousand taka); (c) Courts of Magistrates of the third class: Imprisonment for a term not exceeding (two years) and Fine not exceeding (two thousand taka) (*ibid*, s.32,). Chief Metropolitan Magistrate (Chief Judicial Magistrate or any Additional Chief Judicial Magistrate) can try as a Magistrate all offences not punishable with death; Metropolitan Magistrate or any Magistrate of the first class with power to try as a Magistrate all offences not punishable with death or with transportation or with imprisonment for a term exceeding ten years. (*ibid*, s. 29C). It is said earlier that judicial magistrate courts have been separated from the executive since 1st Nov. 2007. Therefore, what performance has been shown by these courts in the period (2008-2016) is a matter of research. In order to determine the role of the mentioned courts in the said period, it requires presenting a comparative yearly basis data on the number of filing and disposal cases in the mentioned courts:

Table No.5.2: Number of Filing & Disposal of Cases by the Judicial Magistrate Courts during the Period (2008-2016)

Year	Filing New Cases	Disposal of Cases	Remarks
2008	7,58,578	4,42,725	Disposal < Filing
2009	5,92,008	4,62,235	Disposal < Filing
2010	7,41,838	7,09,112	Disposal < Filing
2011	7,06,069	6,71,628	Disposal < Filing
2012	8,00,282	7,25,523	Disposal < Filing
2013	7,51,180	6,62,022	Disposal < Filing
2014	7,92,433	7,34,359	Disposal < Filing
2015	7,76,181	8,47,398	Disposal > Filing
2016	7,32,049	7,80,805	Disposal > Filing

Source: Annual Reports, 2008-2016, HCD, Supreme Court of Bangladesh

From the above table it is clear that disposal rate was lesser than filing of cases in first seven years (2008-2014) after separation whereas in the years 2015-2016, it is more than filing of cases. In the end of year-2007, there were 6, 18,671 cases as pending in the magistrate courts (Annual Report, HCD, 2008) but at the end of year-2016, the number of pending cases stood as 8,65,536 (Eight Lakh Sixty Five Thousand Five Hundred Thirty Six). As a result, new backlog of cases in this period stands as 2,46,865 (Two Lakh Forty Six Thousand Eight Hundred Sixty Five) (Annual Report, HCD, 2008 & 2016).

Figure No.5.3: Trend of Filing and Disposal Rate in the Judicial Magistrate Courts during the Period (2008-2016)

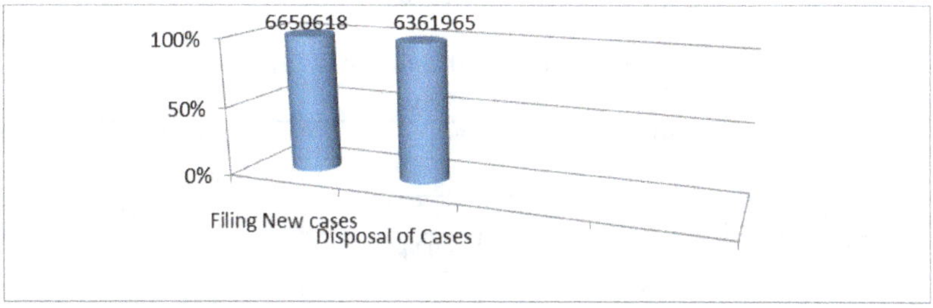

Source: Table 5.2

It is evident from the above table and figure said that 95.65% (63, 61, 965) have been disposed of among filing cases 66,50,618 excluding pending cases of previous years (before 2008) in the period (2008-2016). The trend of filing, disposing of and pending of cases can be exposed in the following figure:

Figure No.5.4: Trend of Filing, Disposal and Pending of Cases by Judicial Magistrate Courts in the Period (2008-2016)

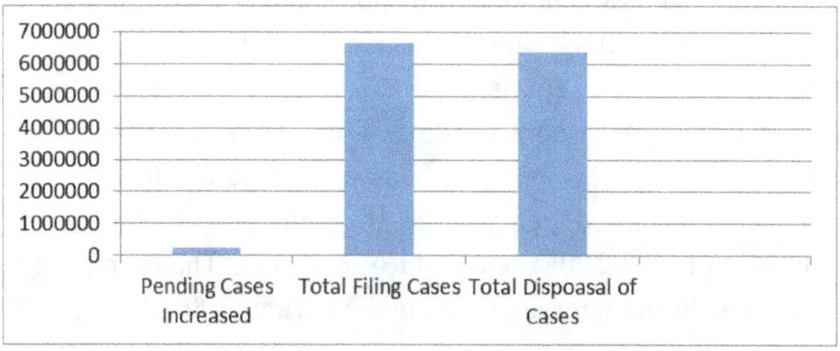

Source: Table 5.2

5.2.3 The Role of Higher Judiciary

The Constitution empowers the HCD as custodian to protect the citizens' fundamental rights (Article 44) and upgrade the rule of law in the country by applying judicial review conferred upon Article 102 of the constitution to examine the activities of the executive legislature and even lower judiciary with a view to ensuring citizens' rights and establishing the rule of law. Generally, writ bench of the higher judiciary is empowered to discharge these responsibilities. The performance of the writ court in the separation subsequent period (2008-2016) is as under:

Table No.5.3: Number of Filing and Disposal of Writs in Writ Courts during the Period (2008-2016)

Year	Filing New writs	Disposal of Writs	Remarks
2008	11,402	8915	Disposal < Filing
2009	8,848	6370	Disposal < Filing
2010	10,175	7303	Disposal < Filing
2011	11,421	10924	Disposal < Filing
2012	17,876	8028	Disposal < Filing
2013	12,958	7473	Disposal < Filing
2014	12843	8688	Disposal < Filing
2015	14,284	13457	Disposal < Filing
2016	16,965	9857	Disposal < Filing

Source: Annual Reports, 2008-2016, HCD, Supreme Court of Bangladesh

From the above table, one thing is revealed that the number of disposal of writs is lesser than number of filing writs in each year particularly from the year-2008 to year- 2016. At the end of year-2007, there were 40,980 (Forty Thousand Nine Hundred Eighty) writs as pending for disposal and the total number of pending writs stands as 69,326 (Sixty Nine Thousand Three Hundred Twenty Six) at the end of year-2016 (Annual Reports, 2008-2016, High Court Division). Therefore, in the period (2008-2016) new pending writs stand as 28346 (Twenty Eight Thousand Three Hundred Forty Six). On an average about 3150 new pending writs have been increased per year in the said period whereas in the pre-separation period (1972-2008) it was 1139 per year. Therefore, the number of pending writs has been increased thrice in the period (2008-2016).

Figure No.5.5: Trend of Filing and Disposal Rate in Writ Courts during the Period (2008-2016)

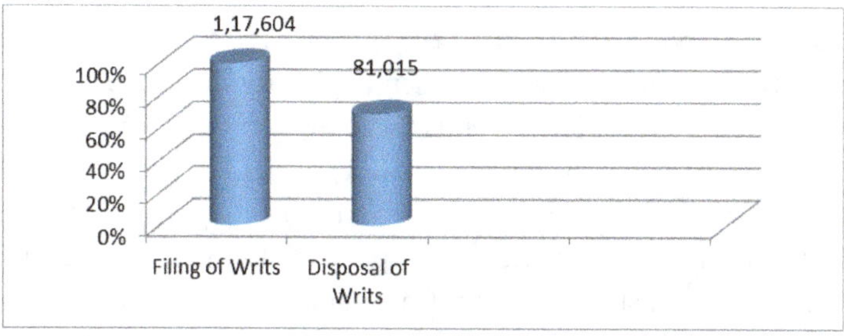

Source: Table No. 5.3

It is found from the above Table No. 5.3 and Figure No. 5.5 that 68.89% writs have been disposed of in the period (2008-2016) excluding the pending writs of pre-separation period (1972-2007).

Figure No.5.6: Comparative Trend of Pending Cases in Magistrate, Civil & Writ Courts at the End of 2007 and at the End of 2016

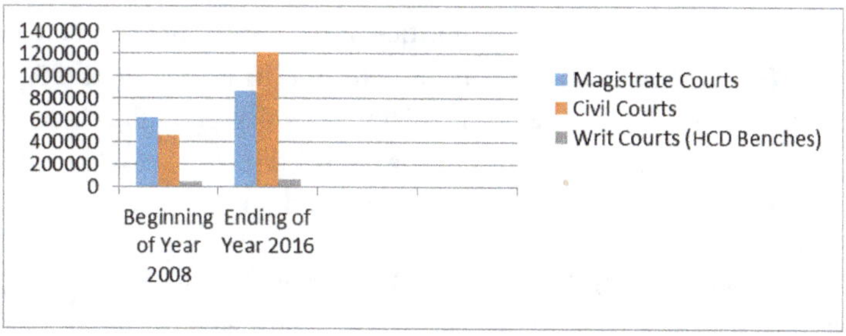

Source: Table No. 5.1, 5.2 & 5.3

From the graph it is very clear that the number of pending cases has become almost twice in the period (2008-2016) and therefore, the citizens' sufferings has been increased automatically and justice delayed or the affected citizens are getting back their infringed rights from the courts in delay which means justice is denied and under these circumstances the rule of law may not be upgraded.

5.3 The Rule of Law in Judicial Pronouncements

The judiciary is discharging its onerous responsibility of by disposing the cases and giving judicial pronouncements in which the spirit of rule of law is reflected. Several relevant cases disposed and uttered judicial pronouncements by the Judiciary in the period (2008-2016) have been selected and studied in order to determine the role of judiciary in upgrading the rule of law as under:

In the case of Habib Khan v State **(2012) 64 DLR 462** it is held by the HCD that the court can certainly interfere when the liberty of a citizen is taken away and the freedom of right of a citizen is taken away by the subordinate court. In the leading case ***BLAST v Bangladesh*** **(2011) 63 DLR 1** the court declared the imposition and execution of extra judicial punishment by the name of Fatawa as void, having no legal effect without proper lawful authority and violative of fundamental rights enshrined in the Constitution. The Court also gave some directions to be implemented by the government to prevent the imposition and execution of extra judicial punishment by the name of Fatawa from the society. In the case of ***HRPB v Bangladesh*** **(2011) 63 DLR 71** it is opined that the government is bound to protect life and property of the people in the discharge of its constitutional obligation; the Government has been directed to make available sufficient necessary equipment for rescue of the citizens soon after occurrence of a severe earthquake. In the case of ***BLAST v Bangladesh*** **(2011) 63 DLR 643** the higher judiciary declared corporeal punishment as absolutely prohibited, inflicting it be deemed as misconduct of the concerned teachers, and gave directions to the concerned authorities of the Government to take necessary steps. In ***Ain-o-Salish Kendra v Bangladesh*** **(2011) 63 DLR 95** the court declared child workers aged between 8-16 years working in the 'Bidi' Factories as illegal and unconstitutional and gave some directions to the government authority to ensure compulsory education for children.

In the case of ***State v Anjali Devi*** **(2009) 61 DLR 738** the HCD re-established the right of citizens to fair trial. The lower court gave death penalty to the condemned prisoner/ accused appellant, Anjali Debi alias Monju Devi under section 6(1) of the Nari-o-Shishu Nirjatan Daman Ain, 2000 for human trafficking though the HCD found that the prosecution proved the case of abduction in the negative way but not the case of trafficking. The HCD also said in their judgment that for this offence the court could award lesser sentence and warned the learned Judge of trial court.

In the case of ***Emdadul Haque v DG, Education*** (2008) 60 DLR the court gave decision that the withdrawal of the name of the petitioner from the MPO list without giving any notice and affording an opportunity of being heard to the petitioner is a clear violation of the principle of natural justice; and is of no legal effect; the respondents was directed to pay the petitioner the MPO salary from May, 2008. In the case of ***Z. I. Khan Panna*** v ***Bangladesh & ors*** (2016) 7

SCOB HCD 7 it is held that the law-enforcing agencies cannot take the law into their own hands. It is also held that in a writ proceeding under Article 102 adequate compensation can be awarded to the victims of human rights violations in the custody of law enforcing agency/ joint forces. In the case of ***AKM Shafiuddin v Bangladesh*** (2012) 64 DLR 508 an important direction is given on the doctrine of separation of power and judicial review as follows in the Para 33 of the Judgment:

> "Every organ is free to act in its own field according to powers conferred on it. If it is not done and one organ transgresses the limit, there is a provision of the Constitution under Article 102 whereby a judicial review of its action is possible. It is the Judiciary which is entrusted with the task of keeping every organ of the State within the limits of law. Any attempt by the legislature to usurp the judicial function is ultra vires."

5.4 Reasons behind Poor Performance and Failure to Upgrade the Rule of Law in the Said Period

In order to discharge the constitutional responsibility and ensure and upgrade the rule of law in the country, the judiciary was separated in 2007 but in the research period (2008-2016) it is revealed in the previous sections of the paper that the judiciary could not show better performances. Under these circumstances the reasons are identified as under:

Ineffective Separation of Powers

According to the Article 109 of the Constitution the High Court Division has control and superintendence over all subordinate courts and tribunal in the country but present Articles 115 & 116 make an obstacle to the higher judiciary in exercising such powers as these Articles declare that the appointment, posting, promotion and grant of leave and discipline of persons employed in the judicial service and magistrates exercising judicial functions shall be exercised by the President in consultation with the Supreme Court. This dual rule system prevents quick appointment, posting of the judicial officers in the sub-ordinate courts or lower judiciary at district level where there are vacancies of judicial officers which creates complexity and delay in providing justice to the citizens and establishing the rule of law in the society.

Shortage of Judges/ Inadequate of Number

At the end of 2016 the number of pending cases stands about 3.16 million over the judiciary and the main reason behind it is inadequate number of judges in comparing with total population of the country; it is revealed when a comparison is drawn as under:

Table No.5.4: Comparative data on judicial officers

Name of Country	Number of Judges per 10 Lakh Citizens
USA	107
Canada	75
UK	51
Australia	41
India	18
Bangladesh	10

Source: Law Commission

Double Judiciary

The trial by mobile courts held by the executive magistrates creates double judiciary and raise questions among the people as regards the independence of judiciary in the country and such trials often violate rights of citizens (The Daily Star, 6th Aug. 2015) due to not ensuring the fair and open trial enshrined in Article 35 of the Constitution; it is an indirect interference by the executive with the functions of judiciary under which the Judiciary cannot upgrade the rule of law unless mobile court comes to direct supervision of the higher judiciary.

Lack of Digital Approach

Our trial system is based on analogue system; there is lack of digital approach in case of maintaining digital recording of the cases, examining the witness through video conferences etc. It is a matter of hope that digital application has been started in the Supreme Court activities. Latest case judgments and cause list of the Supreme Court are appeared on the Supreme Court website-www.supremecourtbd.com. If digital methods are applied in trial system, the disposal rate of cases will be increased rapidly.

District Headquarter Based Subordinate Judiciary

Currently the subordinate judiciary including upazilla based courts is giving service from the district headquarters; here only financial capable people come rather poor victims. Therefore, poor victims are depriving of access to justice by which rule of law may not be upgraded unless few necessary courts are established at the upazilla level. It is apt to state that assistant judge court or magistrate court worked for seven years at upazilla level before withdrawing them in 1992 and still few courts are working at about fourteen upazillas.

Absence of Separate Investigation Cell

It is apt to say that only disposal of cases is not ensuring justice and upgrading the rule of law. It is often seen in the criminal proceedings that the accused are getting acquittal due to want of proper evidence and proof against him. The main reason behind this is absence of separate investigation cell under the Judiciary and consequently a fair, creditable and quick investigation is not possible where the police are more interested to arrest the accused than to present witnesses (The Daily Ittefaq, 25th Dec. 2016); under this circumstance, evidences are being spoilt. It is also seen in a NHCR survey that the conviction rate is only 10% among the cases at the trial stages (Daily Star, 24th December, 2011). Besides, the witnesses are also not interested to give evidence against the accused due to lack of security.

Old and Backdated Laws

The judiciary is facing problems from backdated laws in ensuring and upgrading the rule of law. Most of the basic laws regarding trial and disposal of cases are backdated, can be said British period laws (As for example, The Code of Criminal Procedure, 1898, The Evidence Act, 1972, The Code of Civil Procedure Act, 1908, The Limitation Act, 1908, The Contract Act, 1872, The Penal Code, 1860 etc.) which are not suitable at the present time. In order to ensure quick disposal of cases by the Judiciary the procedural laws, especially the Code of Criminal Procedure, 1898, the Evidence Act, 1972, the Code of Civil Procedure Act, 1908 are to be updated and reformed and introduced quick alternative disposal process to draw the people in bringing their disputes to the courts. The then chief justice said that "under the present judiciary system people could not get justice immediately or quickly; even 2nd or 3rd generation of them might get it which was totally doing fun with them; the whole system should be changed" (The Prothom Alo, 3rd April, 2016).

Absence of Financial Independence

Officially the judiciary is separated from the Executive in 2007 but the judiciary has no financial independence due to having no self-fund of it; the revenue coming from the court fees are deposited to the Govt. fund; the Judiciary has to depend on the government and the govt. what amount allocated for judiciary each year for the development of judiciary is inadequate (The Prothom Alo, 29th June, 2016). In the financial year-2016, only 112 cores were allocated for judiciary which was very poor for infrastructure development of the judiciary but the govt. earns more from court fees. And under these circumstances, the then chief justice also urges for financial independence of the judiciary so that the judiciary can discharge its onerous responsibility to upgrade the rule of law (The Prothom Alo, 27th January, 2016).

Lack of Adequate Accommodation

The Judiciary-either higher or lower both face extremely accommodation crisis. At 2016 170 judicial officers were sharing the court-room by shifting which interrupts the judicial activities and waste the judicial working hours (BD CJ, 2016). Besides, the government often creates new special courts- woman and child torture prevention tribunal, Speedy Trial Tribunal, Environment Court, Land Survey Tribunal, Labour Tribunal, and Administrative Tribunal etc under existing and new laws without considering the distinct establishment for them which also creates accommodation crisis for judicial officers and hamper their regular activities and makes slow the disposal rate of the cases where the citizens suffer lots and gradually lose their confidence upon the judiciary and rule of law.

Interference by the executive

If the pending cases are withdrawn on political consideration by executive order without fair trial by competent courts, rule of law in the society may not be upgraded by the judiciary; people will lose confidence upon the judiciary. In 2009 a national committee was formed under the then law minister to withdraw cases on political consideration. This committee had recommended 7111 cases including murder cases as politically motivated for withdrawal (Daily Star, 6 August, 2013). Thus principles of rule of law are not maintained where the principle of fair trial in the open court by the competent court is interfered by the executive.

Concluding Remarks

The onerous responsibility of the judiciary to dispose of disputes brought before it between individual and individual, individual and state and individual and different organs of the state without any discrimination, by law and under law; the judiciary is also assigned to examine the activities of the executive, legislature or even the activities of lower judiciary to upgrade the rule of law in the country. Accordingly, in the paper in an inquiry to evaluate the role of the judiciary in upgrading the rule of law in post separation period (2008-2016) it is found that total disposal rate was very poor or lesser than filing of cases except the disposal rate of cases in judicial magistrate courts for last two years (2015-2016) (see Table No. 5.1, 5.2 & 5.3). As a result, the number of pending cases has been increased rapidly in civil courts, judicial magistrate courts and even in writ courts in the said period. At the end of year-2007 the pending cases were 4, 56,604 in civil courts, 6,18,671 in magistrate courts and 40,980 in writ courts whereas it stands as12,05,254 in civil courts, 865536 in judicial magistrate courts and 69,326 in writ courts respectively at the end of year-2016.

In the pre-separation period (1972-2007) the total numbers of pending cases in the mentioned three courts were 1.12 million for 36 years and on an average, it was 30,993 (Thirty Thousand Nine Hundred Ninety-Three) per year whereas in the period (2008-2016) it is 1.02 million for only nine years and on an average it is 1,13, 762 (One Lakh Thirteen Thousand Seven Hundred Sixty-Two) per year. It can be said that the number of pending cases has increased rapidly more than twice or in some cases thrice in the said period which is not helpful to upgrade the rule of law in the country. Under these circumstances, the judiciary could not upgrade the rule of law in the society; the consequence of which the terms 'a society of absence of justice' come in the news of newspapers, talk shows of TV Channels and discussions of the people though it is also revealed in the paper that in several judicial pronouncements that the judiciary has shown positive role in upgrading the rule of law in the country in the said period (2008-2016).

The ineffective separation of power & independence of judiciary, double judiciary, shortage of judicial officers, lack of separate investigation cell under the judiciary, backdated laws, dual rule, analogue system, inadequate accommodation and slow infrastructure development, are actively responsible for the failure of the judiciary in upgrading the rule of law in the said period.

An independent Judiciary is important for preserving the rule of law which allows citizens to seek protection of their rights and redress against government actions (61 DLR 565). It can also be said that in the language of Mr. Ajmal Hossain, 61 DLR 532 opined in the same case that it (An independent Judiciary) is also necessary for guardianship of the constitution and for the establishment of the rule of law. But at the same time it should be kept in the mind of each citizen that the Judiciary alone cannot establish the rule of law in the country except the positive performance of other two organs as it does not possess a magic wand. Besides, rule of law means all organs of a State shall maintain the rule of law (8SCOB AD1).

Chapter 6:

Judiciary and Citizens' Right to Life, Liberty and Right against Inhuman Treatment or Punishment in Bangladesh[297]

Introduction:

Judiciary is an important organ of the state assigned to protect, enforce citizens' rights and to establish the rule of law. Such organ is the custodian and protector of the citizens' rights including the right to life or liberty and right against inhumane treatment or punishment (8 SCOB AD1). The term 'judiciary' refers to all courts and tribunals of a country. Bangladesh judiciary can be classified broadly into (i) the Supreme Court of Bangladesh (The Constitution of the People Republic of Bangladesh, Art. 94) (hereinafter as the Constitution) and (ii) the subordinate courts (the Constitution, Art. 114); The Supreme Court is the highest court in Bangladesh having two branches (a) High Court Division (hereinafter as HCD) and (ii) Appellate Division (hereinafter as AD). The onerous responsibility of the Supreme Court is to protect citizens' fundamental rights including right to life, liberty and right against inhumane treatment or punishment enshrined in Part-III of the Constitution. The Supreme Court is empowered and guaranteed by the Constitution (Art. 44 & 102) to protect such rights. The subordinate courts are lower judiciary consisting of district civil, criminal or special courts. They are also assigned by the existing general laws of the country to provide remedies for protecting and enforcing citizens' non-fundamental legal rights relating to life, liberty or right against inhumane treatment or punishment. It is apt to state that generally the subordinate courts can give remedies available under the general laws for the infringement of non-fundamental rights and that the Supreme Court can enforce citizens' fundamental rights including right to life, liberty and right against inhuman treatment or punishment. It is also important to state here that the Supreme Court can also give remedies for the infringement of non-fundamental rights if all alternative remedies are exhausted (66 DLR 475). Therefore, it can be said that the higher judiciary can issue writ orders for the enforcement of fundamental rights as well as of non-fundamental legal rights (64 DLR (AD)

[297] The author depends in conducting this chapter upon his PhD thesis titled 'Judiciary and Citizens Rights: Bangladesh Perspective (Not-Published) and the published journal paper titled 'The Recent Role of Bangladesh Judiciary in Enforcing Right to Life, Liberty, and against Inhuman Punishment: A Study'.2017. II(II) BiLD Law Journal 19-40.

152). Bangladesh Judiciary was officially separated in 1st Nov.2007. In the separation subsequent years particularly in the period (2008-2016) what is the role of the judiciary in protecting and enforcing citizens' rights special reference to right to life, liberty and right against inhuman treatment or punishment, a matter of research.

6.1. Citizens' Rights: Right to Life, Liberty or Right against Inhuman Treatment or Punishment

The people of a country as citizens are entitled to the rights declared by the supreme law and under general laws of the country where some rights known as citizens' fundamental legal rights; some known as non-fundamental legal rights. Whether citizens' fundamental or non-fundamental rights are recognized and enforced by laws of the country including the supreme law of the land, the citizens of a country as human being are morally entitled to claim human rights for their growth as human beings. But all human rights are not recognized and enforced by law in a country; the recognition, protection and enforcement of some human rights in the Constitution of a country turns them into citizens' fundamental rights or civil & political rights. Right to life, liberty and right against inhumane treatment or punishment right to movement, right to speech, right to association are examples of such rights; some human rights are also recognized in the constitution of a developing country like Bangladesh, India, Pakistan etc but they are not enforced; they only get priority in taking state policy.

Right to life may be said as the most important right of each citizen of a country as all other rights are accruing and surrounding it. It is an indispensible right of all human being whether he is citizen of a country or stateless people. Universal Declaration of Human Rights, 1948, Article 3 declares that everyone has the right to life, liberty and security of person. ICCPR, 1966, Article 6(1) states: "Every human being has the inherent right to life. This right shall be protected by law. No one shall be arbitrarily deprived of his life." Such right is recognized and ensured to the citizens of Bangladesh under Bangladesh Constitution by Articles 31 and 32. Article 32 provides that no person shall be deprived of his life and personal liberties save in accordance with law. Lawful deprivation of life is only justifiable when it is needed to ensure safety, security and personal liberty in the society so that individual citizens can enjoy their life and liberty. Death sentence is valid when it is given to protect the lives of other citizens in the society (Islam, 2012, P. 271). A citizen cannot deprive of his right to life or liberty even in imprisonment or detention (*Ibid*, P. 261). And no action detrimental to life shall be taken except in accordance with law (Art. 31). No one can expect that the state should provide livelihood (means of living) rather citizens think that state should not take any action or pass any unreasonable law containing inhumane punishment and causing detrimental to his livelihood as livelihood is covered by the term right to life (*Ibid*, P. 255).

The right to life is also explained in several judicial pronouncements by the Supreme Court of Bangladesh and the ambit of such right is being frequently expanded. In BJMAS v. Ministry of Home Affairs 2008 BLD 580 it is explained as 'the right to life' includes right to security of life which is interpreted as security against natural disasters like earthquake in another case (63 DLR 71). Before these two judicial pronouncements the terms 'right to life' was explained as 'right to protection of health and normal longevity' in a judicial pronouncement (48 DLR 438) and in another as 'right to sound mind & health' (52 DLR 413). Such right may be right to protection and improvement of environment (55 DLR 69); right to a decent and healthy way of life in a hygienic condition; it also means a qualitative life from environmental hazards (*ibid*). Another inclusion we found in 'right to life' in another judicial pronouncement as right to environment and ecology **(65 DLR (AD) 181)**.

Personal liberty means the freedom of an individual to act as he or she wishes except lawful restraint by law (Black's Law Dictionary). Each citizen has right to personal liberty for his smooth living in the society (Article, 9 ICCPR, 1966). Article 10, ICCPR, 1966 requires anyone deprived of liberty to be treated with dignity and humanity. If his right is wrongfully restrained by any other individual, group of people, law forces or by even State herself, he or she or his representative can take legal action. Even the HCD can sou moto interfere when it comes to its knowledge that liberty of a citizen had been taken away by the unlawful ground by the order of the subordinate court (64 DLR 462).

The constitution guarantees the citizens and non-citizens of Bangladesh from inhuman treatment and punishment as per Art.35 (5) by saying, "No person shall be subjected to torture or to cruel, inhuman, or degrading punishment or treatment". The same view is reflected in Article 7, ICCPR, 1966. The higher judiciary also gave rule against torture or to cruel, inhuman treatment or punishment. In this point the HCD held that the very system of remand with a view to interrogation and seeking information by application of force is totally against the spirit and clear provision of the Constitution (55 DLR 363).

6.2. The Recent Role of Judiciary

The judiciary is assigned to protect citizens' rights (fundamental and non-fundamental legal rights) including right to life, liberty and equal protection of law under constitutional law (Articles 44 & 102) and general laws of the country and uphold the rule of law. It is rightly said that the Judiciary is the custodian and protector of the citizens' rights (8 SCOB AD1). A citizen can go to the HCD for the enforcement of his fundamental rights including right to life, liberty and equal protection of law directly under Article 102 (1) of the Constitution. He can also go for the enforcement of non- fundamental legal rights under Article 102(2) subject to exhaustion of all efficacious remedies available under general laws in lower judiciary (66 DLR 475). Even a citizen can bring a petition before the Court under Article 102 for the enforcement of fundamental rights though his rights are not directly and personally affected through public interest litigation.

In a case the Appellate Division gave an *obitur dictum* that when any violation of fundamental rights enshrined in the Constitution was alleged as the only ground and no violation of legal right or any provision of law protecting citizen's right was raised, only then resort may be taken to fundamental rights to protect any citizen of such right (61 DLR (AD) 28).

It is pertinent to mention that the higher judiciary cannot give remedies against the violation of rights by a private individual or private corporation, institution etc. In this case, citizens can seek remedies from subordinate district civil or criminal courts under general laws viz. Penal Code, Specific Relief Act. District criminal courts either session courts or judicial magistrate courts can try offences affecting citizens' right to life, liberty and right against inhumane treatment or punishment enshrined in the criminal laws existing in Bangladesh.

The above discussion conveys the theoretical approach regarding the role of the judiciary (both-higher and lower) in protecting citizens' rights where data based study will give a practical role of the judiciary on citizens' rights. Under this circumstance, a data based study regarding number of filing and disposal of cases in the District Session Judge Courts, Equivalent Special Criminal Courts & Tribunals and Judicial Magistrates' Courts in recent years particularly in the period (2008-2016) will convey an idea on the recent role of the judiciary:

Table No.6.1: Number of Filing and Disposal of cases, in the District Session Judge Courts, (Equivalent Special Criminal Courts & Tribunals) and Judicial Magistrates' Courts in the Period (2008-2016)

	District Session Judge Courts (including equivalent special criminal courts & tribunal)		**Judicial Magistrates Courts**	
Year	**Filing New Cases**	**Disposal of Cases**	**Filing New Cases**	**Disposal of Cases**
2008	159403	131988	7,58,578	4,42,725
2009	159290	125076	5,92,008	4,62,235
2010	195618	149928	7,41,838	7,09,112
2011	219226	161366	7,06,069	6,71,628
2012	269785	198551	8,00,282	7,25,523
2013	261792	191730	7,51,180	6,62,022
2014	314624	219336	7,92,433	7,34,359
2015	358697	265200	7,76,181	8,47,398
2016	348995	278631	7,32,049	7,80,805
Total	2382043	1552981	66,50,618	60,35,807

Source: Annual Reports, 2008-2016, High Court Division, Supreme Court of Bangladesh

It is revealed from the above table that within the period (2008-2016) total numbers of filing cases in all sessions' courts are 2382043 whereas the total number of disposal of cases in mentioned courts are 1552981. At the end of year-2016 the total pending cases in session courts stand as 647422 (excluding transfer cases) whereas it was 253832 (excluding transfer cases) in the beginning of the year-2008 (Annual Reports, 2008 & 2016, HCD, Supreme Court of Bangladesh). As a result, in the mentioned period (2008-2016) new pending cases stand as (647422-253832) =393590 (excluding transfer cases) whereas it was 253832 (excluding transfer cases) from the year 1972-2007 for last 36 years (Annual Reports, 2008 & 2016, HCD, Supreme Court of Bangladesh). So the trend of pending cases in the said period (2008-2016) is about twice in comparison with previous period (1972-2007). It is also revealed that in the judicial magistrate courts 66,50,618 cases have been filed in the said period (2008-2016) but 60,35,807 cases have been disposed of in the mentioned period. At the beginning of year-2008 the total pending cases in the judicial magistrate courts were 618671 (excluding transfer cases) which have stood as 865536(excluding transfer cases) at the end of year 2016(Annual Reports, 2008 & 2016, HCD, Supreme Court of Bangladesh). Therefore, within the said period (2008-2016) new pending cases have been increased as 246865. This new pending cases have been added to the old list of pending cases in the judicial magistrate courts like session courts. Such data analyses regarding pending cases in criminal courts convey the message that the judiciary has not shown better performance in ensuring the criminal justice to the citizens comparatively in the recent years. As a result, it can be said that affected citizens whose right to life or liberty under threat or pressure or violated have not got quick relief under general criminal laws from the criminal courts in the recent years particularly in the period (2008-2016).

Right to life, liberty and right against inhumane treatment or punishment are citizens' fundamental rights. If they are affected exclusively and if no question of violation of legal right or any provision of law protecting citizen's right to life or liberty was raised under general laws, aggrieved citizens can go to the HCD and bring an action in the form of habeas corpus writ for the enforcement of their right to life or liberty. Under these circumstances by considering the number of filing and disposal of writs in Writ Courts (HCD Benches) in the recent years particularly in the period (2008-2016), we can get an idea regarding the role of the judiciary on ensuring and protecting citizens' right to life, liberty and right against inhumane treatment or punishment which are as under:

Table No.6.2: Number of Filing and Disposal of writs in Writ Courts in the Period (2008-2016)

Year	Writ Courts (HCD Benches)		Remark
	Filing New writs	Disposal of Writs	Disposal Rate
2008	11,402	8915	Disposal < Filing
2009	8,848	6370	Disposal < Filing
2010	10,175	7303	Disposal < Filing
2011	11,421	10924	Disposal < Filing
2012	17,876	8028	Disposal < Filing
2013	12,958	7473	Disposal < Filing
2014	12843	8688	Disposal < Filing
2015	14,284	13457	Disposal < Filing
2016	16,965	9857	Disposal < Filing
Total	1,16,772	81,015	Disposal < Filing

Source: Annual Reports, 2008-2016, HCD, Supreme Court of Bangladesh

It is evident from the above table that disposal rate was lesser than filing rate of writ in the writ courts per year. In the said period (2008-2016), total 116772 writs have been filed whereas only 81015 writs have been disposed of. At the end of year-2016 the total pending writs in the writ courts stand as 69326 whereas it was 40980 in the beginning of the year-2008(Annual Reports, 2008

& 2016, HCD, Supreme Court of Bangladesh). As a result new pending writs stand as (69326-40980)=28346 in the said period. Therefore, it can be said that within the said period new pending writs stand 28346 for only nine years whereas it was 40980 for last 36 years from the year 1972-2007 (Annual Reports, 2008 & 2016, HCD, Supreme Court of Bangladesh). So, in the recent years, particularly, in the said period, the trend of pending writs has been increased in comparison with previous period (1972-2007). As a result, citizens could not get back their right to life, liberty and right against inhumane treatment or punishment more quickly. It is relevant to mention that within the said period the number of population has also been increased and the number of judges has also been increased but it was inadequate in comparing with developed and developing countries which researcher will discuss in the problems section (section 6).

6.3. Judicial Recent Trends

Whenever the rights of a citizen are affected, it is the constitutional mandate upon the court to adjudicate it and enforce it (Islam, 2012). Because of the Constitution empowers the HCD as custodian to protect the citizens' fundamental rights including right to life, liberty and right against inhuman treatment or punishment (Article 44). And the judiciary is always upgrading and expanding the scope of citizens' rights including right to life, liberty and right against inhuman treatment or punishment. In recent years particularly in the period (2008-2016) the active role of the judiciary in protecting citizens' right to life, liberty and right against inhumane treatment or punishment have been found in several judicial pronouncements.

It is now well settled proposition of law that even the HCD can sou moto interfere when it comes to its knowledge that liberty of a citizen had been taken away by the unlawful ground. In such matter the court should avoid technicality. When the State does not raise any objection in such circumstances, this court can certainly interfere, when the liberty of a citizen is curtailed and his valuable right of freedom is taken away by the order of the subordinate court. The HCD is empowered under section 491 of the Code of Criminal procedure to set at liberty of the victim who is found to be detained illegally or improperly (64 DLR 462).

In another recent leading case the judiciary declares the extra-judicial punishment by the name of execution of Fatwa without proper authority is violation of fundamental rights enshrined in Articles 31, 32, and 35 of the

Constitution and does not have any legal effectiveness (63 DLR 1). In this case it is also decided that the failure of the State to take any systematic action to address to such incidents of imposition and execution of extra judicial penalties involves a breach of its obligation under the Constitution and international law to ensure the right to freedom from cruel, inhuman and degrading treatment or punishment. The following directions have also been issued to prevent extra-judicial punishment by the name of execution of Fatwa:

(a) The persons who by the name of execution of Fatwa impose any extra-judicial punishments and their abettor(s) shall be held responsible under Penal Code and other existing laws in the regard.
(b) The law enforcing agencies and the Union Parishads and the Pourashavas across the country shall take preventive measures and legal steps to stop extra-judicial punishments in the name of execution of Fatwa.
(c) The Ministry of Local Government shall intimate the law enforcing agencies, all the Union Parishads and the Pourashavas across the country that imposition of extra-judicial punishment is beyond the Constitution and is punishable under the law. The Government shall take appropriate steps for creating awareness amongst people regards extra-judicial punishment in the name of execution of Fatwa as impermissible in law and, in fact, a crime.
(d) The Ministry of Education shall give priority in incorporating various articles and educational materials in the syllabus in School, College and University level and particularly in Madrasha level highlighting the supremacy of the Constitution and the Rule of law and discouraging imposition of extra-judicial punishment of any form in the name of execution of Islamic Sharia/Fatwa.

The judiciary has recently given another landmark decision regarding mandatory death in any statute in the case of **BLAST & Others v. Bangladesh & Others (2015) 1 SCOB (AD)1 and *BLAST* v. *Bangladesh* (2011) 63 DLR 10 in which the judiciary** declared mandatory death penalty in any statute as inconsistent with citizens' rights accruing particularly in Articles 27, 31, 32 & 35 of the Constitution and so such provisions are ultra vires the constitution and therefore they are void. The provisions of different statutes like Sub-sections (2) and (4) of section 6 of the Nari-O-Shishu Nirjatan (Bishesh Bidhan) Ain, 1995, subsections (2) and (3) of section 34 of the Nari-O-Shishu Nirjatan Daman Ain, 2000 and section 303 of the Penal Code are declared ultravires the Constitution. It is also declared that there shall be no mandatory sentence of death in respect of an offence of murder committed by an offender who is under a sentence of life imprisonment.

It is also seen in a recent judicial pronouncement the judiciary has shown an important views regarding for protection of citizens' right to life in a severe earthquake time (63 DLR 71). In the case of ***HRPB*** v. ***Bangladesh*** (2011) 63 DLR 71 it is held that the government is bound to protect life and property of the people in the discharge of its constitutional obligation. The Government is therefore directed to make available sufficient necessary equipment for rescue of the citizens soon after occurrence of a severe earthquake. And it is also declared that recent news items published in different national dailies creates great anxiety among the citizens of Bangladesh. Even it is also declared in this case that if further direction is needed, the parties will be at liberty to make applications in the instant rule as this rule nisi will be treated as continuous mandamus.

In the case of ***BLAST*** v. ***Bangladesh*** (2011) 63 DLR 643 the judiciary has upgraded its views regarding the corporeal punishment upon the children in the educational institutions and declared it as violative of Articles 27, 31, 32 and 35 of the constitution. The higher judiciary also declared corporeal punishment as absolutely prohibited, inflicting it be deemed as misconduct of the concerned teachers, and gave directions to the concerned authorities of the Government to take necessary steps to prevent the imposition of corporeal punishment by way of framing and adopting and disseminating appropriate guidelines, directions or orders to all concerned authorities.

The following directions are issued on the demand of emergency:

1. Corporeal Punishment is absolutely prohibited in all educational institutions of the country
2. Giving corporeal punishment to the students shall be treated as misconduct.
3. District Educational Officers and Upazila Secondary Education Officers shall take necessary measures to end corporeal punishment; they shall take steps against the teachers imposing corporeal punishment under the Penal Code, 1860, the Children act, 1974 and where fit by taking departmental steps.
4. Head of the Educational Institutions shall take effective steps to stop corporeal punishment in their institutions.

5. School Management Committee shall take measures for identification of the teachers inflicting corporeal punishment and shall take actions with rules against the concerned teachers accused of corporeal punishment.

6. Inspectors of the concerned offices, departments and board of education under the Ministry of Education shall monitor whether in the educational institutions corporeal punishment is inflicted and shall take necessary steps to stop it in there.

The judiciary gave a milestone views in the case of ***Z. I. Khan Panna*** v. ***Bangladesh & ors*** 7 SCOB (2016) HCD 7 on the right of the victim of custodial death by law enforcing agencies during the period of "Operation Clean Heart" to bring legal action and seek compensation through the writ jurisdiction. It is stated in 75 Para of the Judgment:

"The affected persons/victims of brutalities or torture or the dependants/family members of the deceased in case of custodial deaths during the 'Operation Clean Heart' will be at liberty to file cases against the perpetrators of the crimes, that is to say, the concerned members of the joint forces/law-enforcing agencies both under civil and criminal laws of the land for justice. They may also invoke the writ jurisdiction of the High Court Division under Article 102 of the Constitution for compensation, if they are so advised, in addition to the reliefs sought for under prevalent civil as well as criminal laws of Bangladesh."

The court argued for adequate compensation awarded to the victims of human rights violations in the custody of law enforcing agency/ joint forces. The amount of compensation will vary from case to case upon the facts and circumstances of each case.

In the case of BELA v. Bangladesh (2010) 62 DLR 463 the court recognized the right to protection of law, to life and to hold properties of the villagers guaranteed by the Constitution and urged the respondents to discharge their duties to ensure those rights of the villagers. The court also gave direction upon the respondents to stop illegal extraction of sand from the bed and banks of the river and outside the designated area of the Fazilpur Sand Quarry.

The Judiciary has given another important views on premature death of citizens and their right to life in the case *of* ***Bangladesh Beverage v. Rowshan Akter*** **(2010) 62 DLR 483.** In this case the court said that life is bundle of incident. Every child is born with expectation of life and with constitutional guaranteed rights of basic requirements for living. Death is inevitable but premature death in whatever form is not expected and cannot be consoled. Accidental death is also a premature death. Government is answerable to all such premature death as Government is to protect the citizen and is responsible for the life of a citizen.

6.4. Real Scenario of Citizens' Right to Life, Liberty and Right against Inhumane Treatment or Punishment

In the previous section the active role of the judiciary has been noticed in protecting citizens' right to life, liberty and right against inhumane treatment or punishment in recent several judicial pronouncements but what are the reality in the society to such rights can be realized in the following data:

Table No.6.3: Scenario of Enforced Disappearances of the Citizens in the Recent Years

Year	Number of Victims	Body Discovered	Traced
2017 (Jan-July)	45	2	10
2016	97	11	29
2015	55	8	12
2014	88	23	25
2013	72	5	10
2012	56	4	18
2011	59	16	4
2010	47	6	7
Total	519	75	115

Source: Ain O Salish Kendra

From the above table it is evident that the numbers of enforced disappeared citizens are gradually increasing each year except one or two cases which are giving very alarming message regarding citizens' right to life or liberty.

Table No.6.4: Scenario of Extra Judicial Killing of the Citizens by Law Enforcing Agencies in the Recent Years

Year	Total
2017 (Jan-July)	109
2016	195
2015	192
2014	154
2013	189
Total	730

Source: Ain O Salish Kendra

From the above table it is also revealed that the numbers of extra-judicial killings have been increased per year except 2014 which is also alarming message for citizens regarding their constitutional right to life, liberty and right against inhumane treatment or punishment. Such extrajudicial killings are arbitrary or unlawful deprivation of citizens' life which is not acceptable at any cost in any sort of society. Under these circumstances this year (28.03.17) the United Nations expressed their concern and criticized Bangladesh (in a report on political and civil rights by the UN Human Rights Committee) for a "high rate" of extrajudicial killings and enforced disappearances at the hands of police, RAB and other law enforces. Quoting on this report, Al Jazeera said than more 1300 cases of extrajudicial killings and 325 enforced disappearances traced out since 2009 (en. prothom alo.com, 30 March, 2017). On the other hand, it is often seen on the daily newspapers and heard here and there that the victims are not interested to go to courts for bringing an action due to the presence of culture of not getting justice and severe harassment from the government. Indeed, this is a continuous real scenario regarding citizens' right to life, liberty and right against inhumane treatment or punishment. Even the National Human Rights Commission of Bangladesh can do nothing to investigate such extrajudicial killings by the state actors. Therefore, the UN has expressed concern at the failure to empower the NHRCB to investigate such gross violation of rights of citizens by the state actors and recommended empowering it to probe the complaints of such violation (ibid).

6.5. Problems in Enforcing Citizens' Right

The judiciary is under constitutional obligation to protect and enforce citizens' rights including right to life or liberty. And in the previous sections particularly in judicial recent views (section no.4) it is found that the judiciary has shown its upgrading role in protecting and enforcing citizens' right to life, liberty and right against inhumane punishment; it is also found in the role of judiciary section (section no.3) that the performance of the judiciary was not satisfactory in the said period for the disposal rate of cases being lesser than filing new cases and therefore, backlog of cases are increasing rapidly in the judiciary which are really hampering the judiciary in protecting and ensuring citizens' right to life or liberty and establishing the rule of law. The real problems behind such performance of the judiciary are as under:

a. Inadequate Number of Judicial Officers

Bangladesh is over populated country where the judiciary is extremely suffering from huge backlog of cases (more than 3.16 million of pending cases) with shortage of judicial officers; there are only 1268 judges of approved 1655 posts and having vacancies of 387 posts in the lower judiciary. And there are only 98 judges in the higher judiciary (Sinha, 2016). These numbers of judicial officers are very inadequate with the total number of citizens in Bangladesh and backlog of cases in comparing with the number of judicial officers of developed and developing countries in proportion to their citizens as under in the Table:

Table No.6.5: Comparative data on judicial officers

Name of Country	Number of Judges per 10 Lakh Citizens
USA	107
Canada	75
UK	51
Australia	41
India	18
Bangladesh	**10**

Source: The Speech of Chief Justice, BD at National Judicial Conference, 2016

From the above table it is evident that in Bangladesh the number of judicial officers is so poor because of there are only 10 officers per 10 lakh citizens where it is 18 in India in our neighboring developing country like us; in developed country like USA it is more than 10 times in comparing with us.

b. Absence of Separate Investigation Cell

In Bangladesh there is no separate investigation cell under the judiciary or judicial magistrate courts; the investigation of an offence or accusation is to be assigned to the police officers, who are under the control of State Ministry. They often take huge time in giving a report and often fail to give a strong report. Therefore, the accused get discharged and victim citizens are depriving of justice. It is often seen that police are more interested to arrest the criminals than to submit an investigation report or present witnesses before the court which is directly responsible for not insuring justice to the victim citizens and they often lose the confidence upon the judiciary. In a field survey conducted by the researcher, it is found that among 30 judicial officers 83.33% respondents (25) gave their opinion for separate investigation team under the judiciary for ensuring citizens' rights; only 10% (3) disagreed; and 6.67% (2) made no comments.

c. Backdated Laws on Evidence

Still today in our judiciary the evidence is taken and witnesses are examined under the Evidence Act, 1872 which is not suitable at the present time where digital system should get priority in disposing of the cases. Digital recording system and examining the witnesses through the video conference system should be introduced in the Evidence Act to dispose of the case more quickly. Besides, the examination of witnesses is very lengthy system which is also responsible for delaying justice to the citizens should be updated. Under these circumstances, Bangladesh Supreme Court drafts witness management policy with a view to reducing litigation time and slash backlog of cases and posted it on the SC website on 31 August, 2017(The New Age, 7th Sep. 2017).

d. Lack of Proper Security to the Witnesses

In the criminal cases particularly murder cases or grievous hurt cases the witnesses are not interested to testify before the courts due to lack of security. As a result, the criminals are getting acquittal due to not prove of the allegation against them which is depriving of justice to the victim citizens. Under these circumstances, Bangladesh Supreme Court proposed a policy in the 21-point witness management policy that the vulnerable or threatened witnesses would be examined through video conference (BD SC, 2017).

e. Corruption

The general people cannot keep confidence upon the judiciary due to corruption but fair trail is the citizens' fundamental rights (Art.35). In a NHCR survey it is seen that conviction rate among the cases brought into trial is only 10% - extremely low often due to corruption (The Daily Star, 24th December, 2011). In a seminar, Prof. Abul Barakat, Ex-Chairman, Janata Bank,claimed that "judgments of lower and higher judiciary are selling". Though, it was denied by the present chief Justice Surendra Kumar Sinha. He claimed it would be 5-10% (The Daily Star and the Prothom Alo, 3rd April, 2016). In a field survey conducted by the researcher, similar view was found on corruption in judiciary. It is found that 66.11% (119) respondents among 180 citizens think that a citizen has to face corruption in order to get justice from court; only 23.89% respondents disagreed with this; and 10% respondents made no comments.

f. Lack of Independent Public Service Commission: Govt. Unskilled Lawyers

In Bangladesh, there is no independent public service commission. Therefore, there is no proper recruitment mechanism in appointing public prosecution. Generally, public prosecutors are appointed in political consideration; as a result, inefficient and inexperienced lawyers are being appointed as public prosecutors who are often failing to prove the case and the victim citizens are deprived of getting justice and are losing confidence upon the judiciary. Besides, it is often seen that by using political backing, most of them get involved in corruption to make quick money; they do not present important witnesses or do not produce the required documents. As a result, the accused get acquittal at the final hearing.

g. Lack of Adequate Accommodation

The Judiciary-either higher or lower both face extremely accommodation crisis. At present 170 judicial officers are sharing the court-room by shifting which interrupts the judicial activities and waste the judicial working hours (BD CJ, 2016). Besides, the government often creates new special courts- woman and child torture prevention tribunal, Speedy Trial Tribunal, Environment Court, Land Survey Tribunal, Labour Tribunal, and Administrative Tribunal etc under existing and new laws without considering the distinct establishment for them which also creates accommodation crisis for judicial officers and hamper their regular activities where the citizens suffer lots and gradually lose their confidence upon the judiciary.

Conclusion

The judiciary is under obligation by constitutional laws and general laws to protect and enforce citizens' rights either fundamental or non-fundamental rights including right to life, liberty and right against inhumane treatment or punishment. And the judiciary has upgraded its role in the several judicial pronouncements in recent years particularly in the period (2008-2016) in protecting and enforcing citizens' rights special reference to right to life, liberty and right against inhumane treatment or punishment.

In a recent judicial pronouncement in the case of *Emran Ahmed* v. *Bangladesh* (2012) 64 DLR 462 the judiciary declares that the HCD can sou moto interfere when it comes to its knowledge that liberty of a citizen had been taken away by the unlawful ground. It is also pronounced in the same case that the HCD is empowered under section 491 of the Code of Criminal procedure to set at liberty of the victim who is found to be detained illegally or improperly.

***In the case of BLAST* v. *Bangladesh* (2011) 63 DLR 10 the Judiciary** declared mandatory death penalty in any statute as inconsistent with citizens' rights accruing particularly in Articles 27, 31, 32 & 35 of the Constitution and so such provisions are ultra vires the constitution and therefore they are void.

In the case of ***HRPB*** v. ***Bangladesh*** (2011) 63 DLR 71 the judiciary has shown an important views regarding for protection of citizens' right to life in a severe earthquake time. The Government is directed to make available sufficient necessary equipment for rescue of the citizens soon after occurrence of a severe earthquake.

In the case of ***BLAST*** v. ***Bangladesh*** (2011) 63 DLR 643 the judiciary has upgraded its views regarding the corporeal punishment viz. caning, beating, and chaining upon the children in the educational institutions. The court declared such punishment as prohibited absolutely, and gave directions to the concerned authorities of the Government to take necessary steps to prevent the imposition of corporeal punishment by way of framing and adopting and disseminating appropriate guidelines, directions or orders to all concerned authorities.

Though the judiciary has upgraded its role in protecting and enforcing citizens' rights special reference to right to life, liberty and right against inhumane treatment or punishment in several judicial pronouncements in recent years particularly in the period (2008-2016), it could not show better performance overall in the said period due to the less disposal of cases than filing of cases. As a result, the numbers of pending cases have been increased rapidly (Section No. 3).

At the end of year-2016 the total pending cases in session courts stand as 647422 whereas it was 253832 in the beginning of the year-2008 (Annual Reports, 2008 & 2016, HCD, Supreme Court of Bangladesh). As a result, in the mentioned period (2008-2016) new pending cases stand as 393590.

At the Beginning of year-2008 the total pending cases in the judicial magistrate courts were 618671 which have stood as 865536 at the end of year 2016 (Annual Reports, 2008 & 2016, HCD, Supreme Court of Bangladesh). Therefore, within the said period (2008-2016) new pending cases have been increased as 246865.

At the end of year-2016 the total pending writs in the writ courts stand as 69326 whereas it was 40980 in the beginning of the year-2008(Annual Reports, 2008 & 2016, HCD, Supreme Court of Bangladesh). As a result, new pending writs stand as 28346 in the said period.

So, in the recent years, particularly, in the said period (2008-2016), the trend of pending cases or writs has been increased rapidly in comparison with previous period (1972-2007). As a result, citizens could not get back their infringed right to life, liberty and right against inhuman treatment or punishment more quickly.

Along with the trend of pending cases, the numbers of extra-judicial killings and enforced disappeared citizens are gradually increasing each year in the said period except one or two cases which are giving alarming message regarding citizens' right to life, liberty and right against inhuman treatment or punishment (section no. 5).

Under these circumstances this year (28.03.17) the United Nations expressed their concern and criticized Bangladesh (in a report on political and civil rights by the UN Human Rights Committee) for a "high rate" of extrajudicial killings and enforced disappearances at the hands of police, RAB and other law enforces.

Besides, it is often seen on the daily newspapers and heard here and there that the victims are not interested to go to courts for bringing an action due to the presence of culture of not getting justice and severe harassment from the government. This is a continuous real scenario regarding citizens' right to life, liberty and right against inhumane treatment or punishment where even the

National Human Rights Commission of Bangladesh can do nothing to investigate such extrajudicial killings by the state actors.

The reasons behind the backlog of cases being increased rapidly in the recent years are many (Section No.6):

There is huge vacancy of judicial officers in lower and higher judiciary. Besides, the number of judges in proportionate to the people is very low in comparing with developing and developed countries. As a result, the affected citizens are deprived of getting their rights in due time and are losing their confidence upon the judiciary in spite of its separation from the executive.

The Judiciary are extremely facing accommodation crisis. At present 170 judicial officers are sharing the court-room by shifting which interrupts the judicial activities and waste the judicial working hours.

There is no separate investigation cell under the judiciary or judicial magistrate courts. The judiciary has to depend on Police who are under the control of State Ministry, take huge time to give a report and often fail to give a strong report. Therefore, the accused get discharged and victim citizens are depriving of justice.

Still today, in a case, the evidence is taken and witnesses are examined under the Evidence Act, 1872, which is very backdated laws on evidence in which there is no application of digital system for quick disposal of cases and delivering justice to the affected citizens in due time.

On the contrary, in the criminal cases particularly murder cases or grievous hurt cases the witnesses are not interested to testify before the courts due to lack of security. As a result, the criminals are getting acquittal due to not prove of the allegation against them which is depriving of justice to the victim citizens.

Corruption, inefficiency of govt. lawyers, and lack of public service commission are also responsible for the failure of the judiciary in ensuring and enforcing citizens' rights.

Under the above circumstances, in order to ensure better performance of the judiciary and for ensuring citizens' rights including right to life, liberty and right against inhumane treatment or punishment, the identified problems should be solved; the vacancies of judicial officers should be filled up and the number of judges should be increased in proportionate to the number of citizens with adequate accommodation at least Indian model should be followed here; the law regarding evidence should be updated with ensuring proper security and facilities to the witnesses for their encouragement; separate judicial investigation cell and independent public prosecution service commission should be established; the state actors must stop extra-judicial killings of citizens; if they are notorious criminals, they can be tried by special courts within very short time; and the National Human Rights Commission of Bangladesh can be empowered to investigate such gross violation of rights of citizens by the state actors.

Chapter 7:

Backlog of Cases-Civil & Criminal Justice in Bangladesh[298]

Introduction

Bangladesh judiciary is currently extremely facing the challenge of backlog of cases which is hampering in ensuring civil justice and criminal justice to the litigants; the judiciary are facing crisis of 3.16 million (at the end of 2016) (currently 3.3 million at the end of 2017) pending cases where there is only 1268 judicial officers in the lower judiciary; on an average each judicial officers of the subordinate courts are facing 2143 pending suits along with new cases; in the higher judiciary there is only 98 judges; each of them is facing 4476 backlog of cases per year along with new cases (Ittefaq, 2016). Under these circumstances, the judiciary is failing to discharge its constitutional and legal obligation under Bangladesh Constitution (hereinafter as the Constitution) and the statutory laws. As a result, the people are not getting justice in due time; therefore, they are gradually losing their confidence upon it; they are not interested to bring action to the courts; they often wave their rights or disputed rights which create a culture of absence of justice in the society. In such a society, a father named Hazrat Ali jumped with her daughter on 29th April 2016 in front of a running train near Sreepur Railway Station, Gazipur due to insecurity and injustice (Hasnat, 2017); Prof. Abul Quasem Fazlul Huq, the father of Publisher, Dipan and wife of slain Avijit did not want justice for killing his son or her husband (Khan, 2nd November, 2015, p.1) (Avijit was brutally hacked to death at Dhaka University campus near TSC on 26th February, 2015 while Dipan was killed in similar on 31st October, 2015 at Dhaka's Aziz Supermarket) (Rabbi, 4th Sep. 2016). Under these circumstances, what are the state of civil justice and criminal justice? what are the impacts of backlogs upon the civil and criminal justice are discussed here; the backlog of cases in the lower judiciary before and after the separation of judiciary are also comparatively studied and the problems or challenges behind such huge backlog of cases are also identified.

---

[298] The author depends in conducting this chapter upon his PhD thesis titled 'Judiciary and Citizens Rights: Bangladesh Perspective (Not-Published) and the published journal paper titled 'Backlog of Cases-Civil & Criminal Justice: A Comparative Study-Bangladesh Perspective'. 2019, 6(3), International Journal of Human Rights and Constitutional Studies (IJHRCS), p.214-226.

In Bangladesh, delay is a great problem for which people often forget their rights; they do not want to bring an action in courts as it takes long time to be disposed of. As William Ewart Gladstone said "Justice Delayed is Justice Denied" which is also legal maxim which is also the basis for the right to a speedy trial. Again Justice Reavley said on consequences of delay (cited in Thean, 2003):

> "Delay haunts the administration of justice. It postpones the rectification of wrong and the vindication of the unjustly accused. It crowds the dockets of the courts, increasing the costs for all litigants, pressuring judges to take short cuts, interfering with the prompt and deliberate disposition of those causes in which all parties are diligent and prepared for trial, and overhanging the entire process with the pall of disorganization and insolubility."

Motala (2001) contends for judicial accountability for managing court delay whereas Camion (2016) argues for e-access to justice; Harvard Law Review Association (1978) focuses on the US Speedy Trial Act and Separation of Powers for managing court delay; Alam (2000) draws possible way out of backlog in our judiciary, Law Commission-Bangladesh (2015) argues for the appointment of about 2400 new judges in proportion to the people of the country in comparing with other country.

Since the judiciary especially lower judiciary (judicial Magistrate Courts) was officially separated on 1st Nov.2017 and consequently people should think that judiciary is separate and independent; therefore, in the post separation period how judiciary works: whether the backlogs are reducing? What are states of civil justice and criminal justice in the post separation period; these are all matters of research. And by considering the mentioned matters with a view to further development of the knowledge, this paper has made a comparative study upon backlogs in civil justice and criminal justice; try to find out the problems and challenges behind the backlogs in civil and criminal justice; and consequently some new propositions have been drawn which will create new knowledge and useful for the people of the society, especially for parliament members, academicians, judges, advocates and law students; it will be helpful for making policy to remove the obstacles which are hampering the civil and criminal justice in Bangladesh.

In the present research mixed methodology-analytical and comparative approach have been used; quantitative data collected from the registrar office of the Supreme Court Bangladesh, data also collected by applying the observation method; secondary data are also collected from various source like books, journal articles, online based articles etc. Collected data have been presented with the help of MS Word.

7.1. Backlog of Cases and Civil Justice

Citizens are generally seeking civil justice from the civil courts when their civil rights or individual private rights (rights to property or to post) are violated or denied by any other individuals. In Bangladesh, the subordinate civil courts like Assistant Judge Court, Senior Assistant Judge Court, Joint District Judge Court, Additional District Judge Court and District Judge Courts are assigned to provide civil justice to the affected citizens or litigants. In order to seek civil justice, affected people bring civil suits in the civil courts (civil suit is a suit in which the right to property or post is contested) (The Code of Civil Procedure, 1908, Sec. 9) (hereinafter as CPC). After filing a civil suit, a litigant has to face different stages of a suit and wait for an uncertain time to get justice from court due to the sort of our legal system including adversarial trial system though ADR system having been incorporated as mandatory for quick disposal of civil suits in the CPC in 2012 by the CPC (Amendment) Act 2012. Due to the lengthy trial system and other existing factors (other factors will be discussed in problems section) the disposal rate of civil suits in Bangladesh is generally lesser than filing new suits in each year revealed in the later 'Table No. 7.1. As a result, the number of backlog of cases is gradually increasing per year which is extremely hampering in providing civil justice and consequence of people is losing their confidence upon the judiciary. The state of the performance of the subordinate civil courts in providing civil justice is as under in the table containing number of filing & disposal of suits during the Period (2008-2016) (separation subsequent period):

Table No. 7.1: Number of Filing & Disposal of Suits in the District Civil Courts during the Period (2008-2016)

Year	Filing New Suits	Disposal of Suits	Remarks
2008	1,65,339	1,10003	Disposal < Filing
2009	2,18,275	1,16,711	Disposal < Filing
2010	2,17,537	1,71,604	Disposal < Filing
2011	1,08,689	46,111	Disposal < Filing

2012	2,26,754	58,923	Disposal < Filing
2013	4,36,196	2,36,220	Disposal < Filing
2014	4,33,210	3,22,461	Disposal < Filing
2015	3,32,677	2,66,333	Disposal < Filing
2016	2,43,366	2,24,615	Disposal < Filing

Source: HCD, Supreme Court of Bangladesh, 2008-2016

From the above table it is revealed that in each year from 2008 to 2016 the disposal rate of civil courts was lesser than filing new cases; therefore, the new backlog of cases has lifted up in the said period; under this analysis pending cases of previous years (1972-2007) were not considered; if they are considered, comparative scenario will stand between two periods as under:

Table No. 7.2: Number of Pending Suits in the District Civil Courts during the Periods after Separation (2008-2016) and before Separation (1972-2007)

At the End of Year	**Number of Pending Cases**	**Remarks**
2007	4, 56,604	
2016	12, 05,254	
New Pending Suits	7,48,650	

Source: HCD, Supreme Court of Bangladesh, 2008 & 2016

From the above table it is evident that new pending suits stand in the separation subsequent period as 7, 48,650 (Seven Lakh Forty-Eight Thousand Six Hundred Fifty) which is almost thrice in comparing with previous period of separation. From these data analyses it can be surmised that the trend of providing civil justice was very slow and delay where it is required to identify what are actual reasons or problems behind such performance and such trend of backlog of cases to be discussed in the later section particularly in the problems section.

7.2. Backlog of Cases and Criminal Justice

Subordinate criminal courts viz. District Session Courts, Judicial Magistrate Courts and Special Tribunals are under legal obligation to provide criminal justice to affected people if the public rights are infringed or under threat to be violated. Before the separation of the judiciary executive magistrate courts worked as cognizable courts and trial courts under which the executive had direct interference upon the judiciary at the district level. On 1st Nov. 2007 the executive had lost such power and judicial magistrate courts are now working in place of executive magistrates. Under these circumstances, it is general query of the people of the country how judicial magistrate courts have performed in the separation subsequent period? whether judicial magistrate or sessions courts have any new backlog of cases in the separation subsequent period? whether the confidence of the citizens has upgraded upon the judiciary or not during the said period? In order to get answers to these questions the data regarding number of filing and disposal of cases in criminal courts can be focused as under:

Table No.7.3: Number of Filing and Disposal of cases in the District Session Judge Courts, (Equivalent Special Criminal Courts & Tribunals) and Judicial Magistrates' Courts in the Period (2008-2016)

	District Session Judge Courts (including equivalent special criminal courts & tribunal)			**Judicial Magistrates Courts**		
Year	Filing New Cases	Disposal of Cases	Remarks	Filing New Cases	Disposal of Cases	Remarks
2008	159403	131988	Disposal < Filing	7,58,578	4,42,725	Disposal < Filing
2009	159290	125076	That	5,92,008	4,62,235	That
2010	195618	149928	That	7,41,838	7,09,112	That
2011	219226	161366	That	7,06,069	6,71,628	That
2012	269785	198551	That	8,00,282	7,25,523	That
2013	261792	191730	That	7,51,180	6,62,022	That
2014	314624	219336	That	7,92,433	7,34,359	That
2015	358697	265200	That	7,76,181	8,47,398	Disposal > Filing
2016	348995	278631	That	7,32,049	7,80,805	That
Total	2382043	1552981	That	66,50,618	60,35,807	Disposal < Filing

Source: High Court Division, Supreme Court of Bangladesh, 2008-2016

It is revealed from the above table that in the separation subsequent time the disposal rate is lesser than filing new cases in the session courts whereas the disposal rate in the judicial magistrate courts is also lesser than filing new cases except last two years in the judicial magistrate courts. It is also evident from the table that about 13, 43,873 cases have not disposed of in subordinate criminal courts in comparing between the number of filing and disposal of cases in criminal courts in the said period where one can assume that a huge backlog of cases has newly created in the criminal courts. At the end of year-2016 total pending cases in session courts and judicial magistrate courts stand as 1512958 whereas at the end of 2007 there were total 872503 cases as pending (The Supreme Court of Bangladesh, 2008 & 2016). Therefore, it can be said that pending cases or backlog of cases in the criminal courts stand as double in the mentioned period in comparison with previous period (1972-2007). The trend of backlog of cases in the separation subsequent period can be shown in following figure:

Figure No.7.1: Comparative Trend of Pending Cases in Judicial Magistrates, Session Courts & Civil Courts at the Beginning of 2008 and at the End of 2016

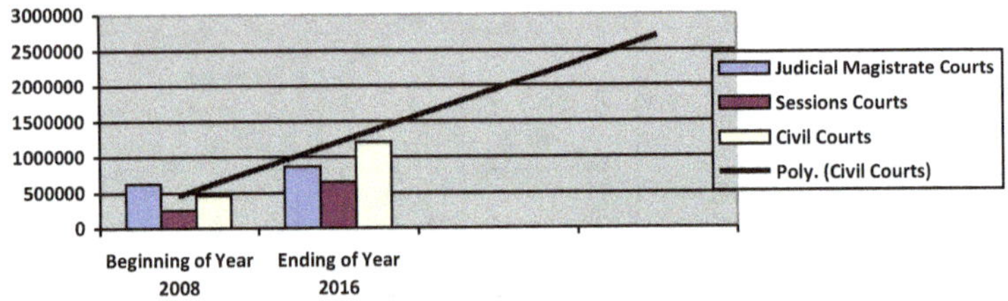

From the graph it is very clear that the number of pending cases has become more than twice in each said courts in the period at the end of 2016 from the year-2008. From the graph it is also revealed that the comparative increasing trend of backlog of cases is highest in the district civil courts. One of the reasons behind such highest backlog of cases in civil courts is severe shortage of judicial officers and appointment of judicial officers as judicial magistrates from the civil courts in the beginning of the separation of judiciary. Such a huge backlog of cases creates overload upon the court and therefore, civil justice and criminal justice are extremely delayed which is a factor of injustice, and also a violator of human rights (Alam,2000). As a result, peoples' sufferings in getting civil or criminal justice are gradually increasing. Therefore, they are losing confidence upon the judiciary which encourages general people and criminals in violating the rights of others and committing severe crimes which we see in the present society and consequently a culture of absence of justice has been created.

7.3. Problems which are creating backlog of cases

The judiciary was separated in 2007 and 10 years have already been passed but backlog of cases are now about 3.3 million, for which one factor is not merely responsible; different factors are directly and indirectly active behind such huge backlogs:

a. District and Session Judge Court System

District and Session Judge Court, Additional District and Session Judge Court or Joint District and Session Judge Court- these courts are disposing of civil and criminal appeal, revision and miscellaneous matters; Joint District Judge Courts are also taking fresh suits of more than Tk. 400000 upto unlimited including suits of NI (Negotiable Instrument) Act where it is seen that these courts are often to be engaged in dealing suits of NI Act; they can give very little attention to disposing of civil suits ; District Judge Court has multi jurisdiction and responsibilities (viz. appeal, revision, review jurisdiction, supervisory jurisdiction etc.). As a result, these courts are always facing overload and consequently, new backlog of cases are increasing extremely. If separate establishment is set for dealing criminal matters by the head of session court, District Judge Court, Additional District Judge Court and Joint District Judge Court or separate establishment for the suits of NI Act can give more concentration to the civil matters and overall, backlog of cases may be reduced.

b. Lengthy Trial System (Adversarial System)

Common law oriented adversarial system is very much lengthy trial system where judges have nothing to do except hearing both parties and recording them. It can be said that parties can play active role in deposing of cases whereas judges are like umpires. But it is often seen that either party lawyer takes time which prolongs the disposal of cases. In order to quick disposal of civil cases alternative dispute resolution (ADR) system has been incorporated as mandatory in the Code of Civil Procedure, 1908 by the CPC Amendment Act, 2012 but it has few reflections as merely a date for ADR being set in cause list. In order to get benefit by ADR mechanism separate court and establishment should be established.

c. Inadequate Judicial Officers or Manpower- stenographers

The lower judiciary is suffering from the crisis of shortage of judicial officers and adequate manpower. There are only 1268 judicial officers against 1655 approved posts in the lower judiciary and 98 (currently 83) in the higher judiciary (Sinha, 2016). These 1366 judicial officers are facing total 3.16 backlogs of cases; on an average each officer has to face 2196 pending cases along with new cases per year (HCD, 2016). Besides, in comparing the number of judicial officers of other developed and developing countries in proportionate of their citizens, the numbers of judicial officers here are also very inadequate in proportion to our citizens. There are 18 judges in India, 107 in USA per 1 million citizens whereas here there are only 10 judges for the same number of citizens (Law Commission-Commission, Bangladesh, 2015). By these poor numbers of judges, it is quite impossible to reduce the backlogs of cases and ensure civil and criminal justice in due time or expected time of litigants. Under these circumstances, Law Commission of Bangladesh proposed in 2015 for appointment of 2400 new judges. Besides, there are no stenographers for assistant and senior assistant judges but they are mainly trial courts in civil justice systems which are also directly responsible of creating backlogs.

d. Dual Rule

Due to the present provisions of the Constitution (Art. 115 & 116) the power of appointment, posting, transfer, promotion of the judicial officers of the subordinate courts are exercised by the President through the ministry of law consultation with the Supreme Court of Bangladesh which creates dual rule in the said issue. But the reality is that the President is bound to act by the advice of the Prime Minister [The Constitution, Art. 48(3)]; that is, the executive has scope to control the judiciary. On the contrary, Article 109 of the constitution gives the HCD of the Supreme Court control and superintendence over lower judiciary. Besides, the original article 116 of the 1972 Constitution had given the Supreme Court power over the lower judiciary which was amended later several times. For this dual rule psychological conflict sometimes arises between the Supreme Court and the ministry of law for which the appointment, posting, transfer, promotion of the judicial officers of the subordinate courts are sometimes extremely hampered which immensely affect the judicial functions and creates backlogs. The former chief justice Surendra Kumar Sinha also claimed it and blamed it for hampering judicial activities (The Daily Star, 1st Nov.2016).

e. Analogue System

Analogue trial system often prolongs civil and criminal justice system and creates backlogs. In order to quick disposal of a case digital methods is to be applied in several cases e.g., maintaining digital recording of the cases, examining the witness through video conferences etc. It is a matter of hope that digital application has been started in the Supreme Court activities. Latest case judgments and cause list of the Supreme Court are appeared on the Supreme Court website-www.supremecourtbd.com.

f. Old & Backdated Laws Laws

Most of the existing laws particularly procedural laws – either civil or criminal or evidence law (i.e.,The Code of Criminal Procedure, 1898, The Evidence Act, 1972, The Code of Civil Procedure Act, 1908, The Limitation Act, 1908, The Contract Act, 1872, The Penal Code, 1860 etc) in the country are much backdated, laws of British regime which are also responsible for backlogs. These laws are not suitable at the present time where digital system should get priority in disposing of the cases. Digital recording system, examining the witness through the video conference system should be introduced in the present trial system to dispose of the case more quickly. Therefore, these laws should be reformed, updated, and digital methods should be introduced and allowed for quick disposal.

g. Absence of Separate Investigation Cell

There is no separate judicial investigation cell where the criminal courts have to depend on the police who are not serious and able to give investigation reports in addition of their regular activities. It is often seen that police are very much interested to arrest criminals than to submit a reliable and credible report; they are often failed to submit a report in due time. And slow and defective investigation process is directly responsible for prolonging the criminal justice and causing failure of providing criminal justice. Even they do not submit witnesses at due time at the time of trial of criminal cases which make the trial slow and lastly the alleged guilty is not proved due to absence of proper witnesses and their evidence (Sinha, 2016).

h. Fake Case

In Bangladesh the numbers of fake cases are significantly increasing in recent years due to different key factors viz. politics, absence of rule of law, habitual litigants etc. There is no accurate statistics on the status of false cases but it is often heard in the seminar, workshop from the concerned persons that 80% of total filing cases in the courts of the country are false. On 23rd June 2013 in seminar the former state law minister Quamrul Islam said that 80% lawsuits of the country are false (Progress Bangladesh, 2013). It is apt to state that in order to prevent false claims there is provisions of compensatory cost in case of civil litigation (CPC, sec.35A & 35B). On the contrary in case of prevention of criminal false case or charges there are several provisions under several enactments like CrPC, sec. 250, the Penal Code, 1860, sec. 211 and the Nari o Sishu Nirjatan Daman Ain 2000, Sec.17. In spite of these laws, the false cases are not stopped which are strongly responsible to create backlogs where they can actually be reduced by the establishment of rule of law, stable political environment, and non-interference from the government etc.

i. Lack of Adequate Accommodation

The lower judiciary was separated in 2007 but still today in many districts the judiciary are facing serious accommodation crisis. As a result, the judicial officers are sharing court room which wastes important judicial hours. At the end of 2016 it is estimated that170 judicial officers are sharing the court-room by shifting which interrupts the judicial activities and waste the judicial working hours (Ittefaq, 2016, p.8). Besides, the government often creates new special courts- woman and child torture prevention tribunal, Speedy Trial Tribunal, Environment Court, Land Survey Tribunal, Labour Tribunal, and Administrative Tribunal etc under existing and new laws without considering the distinct establishment for them which also creates accommodation crisis for judicial officers and hamper their regular activities where the citizens suffer lots and gradually lose their confidence upon the judiciary.

j. Malpractice by lawyers, parties

Generally, the lawyers can play active role in the adversarial system but it is often seen that in some cases lawyers and their parties are playing very inactive role; they are not interested to dispose of the case rather they apply interlocutory matters for lingering the case; they take time for unnecessary causes for their own benefit and prolong the trial and causes backlogs and therefore they are directly responsible for backlog of cases.

7.4. Challenges

The judiciary was separated from the executive on the 1st Nov. 2017 and already 10 years have gone; one of the challenges was at the beginning to ensure true separation and reduce the backlogs of cases but in the subsequent years it is revealed that the backlog of cases are increasing in each year particularly in civil justice system which presently stands as a big challenge. On the contrary, people are losing their confidence upon the judiciary gradually and under these circumstances, it is another big challenge to provide civil and criminal justice in due time:

a. Reducing Backlog of Cases

At the end of year-2016, there were 3.16 million pending cases whereas at the end of 2017, it stands 3.3 million. On the basis of 2016 pending cases statement it is seen that on an average each judicial officer either higher or lower judiciary are facing backlogs of 2116 cases along with new cases. It is apt to mention that in a civil justice system a practice is that each judicial officer is to dispose of 18 cases per three months by both parties hearing and contest. On an average, 64 civil suits are to be disposed of in a year by an officer in both parties contest. As a result, it is quite impossible to reduce backlogs without ensuring strong court management, increasing number of judicial officers & logistic staff (stenographers for the court of assistant judge, and senior assistant judge), separating district and session judge post where senior district judge will hold as district judge and dispose of only civil matters; session judge for criminal matters only, establishing separate ADR courts where a suit is to be filed first for ADR resolution and utilizing mobile SMS facilities in case of summons, ensuring adequate accommodation for judicial officers so that their valuable time are not spared through sharing the court ajlash.

b. Providing Civil and Criminal Justice in Due Time

Under the present trial system with huge overload or backlog of cases it is quite impossible to provide civil or criminal justice in due time. It is also a great challenge for the judiciary to provide civil and criminal justice in due time without recruiting new judicial officers, stenographers, establishing new courts, ensuring proper court management under digital mechanisms.

c. Creating Confidence upon the Judiciary

Under the above mentioned circumstances, it is also a great challenge to enhance the confidence of the citizens upon the judiciary. In order to upgrade citizens' confidence upon the judiciary there is no alternative of ensuring quick delivery of civil justice. And for doing so, incentive system should be considered for more disposals of civil cases along with above recommendations so that judicial officers can be encouraged and motivated and can give more attention and time in disposing of civil suits. It is apt to state that in case of criminal proceeding it takes less time for disposing than civil proceeding; civil proceeding is more complex than criminal proceeding and involved huge documents which require more time, attention for dispose of them. In consequence, same officer when he is engaged in criminal proceedings he is feeling convenient due to sort of nature of criminal proceedings than to civil proceedings. As a result, a psychological trend might be grown among the officers, which make them reluctant and they are feeling inconvenient in disposing of civil suits; the ultimate result is backlogs of cases. Therefore, incentive system should be introduced for disposing of more civil suits and ensuring quick delivery in civil justice system.

Conclusion

Backlog of cases are great problem for the judiciary and consequence of which civil and criminal justice are not possible to be ensured in expected time or in quick time. Therefore, citizens are losing their confidence on the judiciary; they wave their rights; in some cases, they declare openly that they do not want justice due to the existing system and position of the judiciary in providing justice (as Prof. Abul Quasem Fazlul Huq, the father of Publisher, Dipan and wife of slain Avijit claimed so) (Khan, 2nd November, 2015, p.1). In some cases, it is seen that people prefer to suicide than to live due to insecurity and culture of injustice in the society where one Hazrat Ali is burning example (as a father named Hazrat Ali jumped with her daughter on 29th April 2016 in front of a running train near Sreepur Railway Station, Gazipur due to insecurity and injustice) (Hasnat, 6th May, 2017).

From the comparative study of backlogs in civil and criminal justice it is found that the increasing trend of backlogs is highest in the district civil court (see Figure No.1) which extremely hampers delivering of civil justice. At the ending of year-2007 the total number of backlogs in the district civil courts were 4,56, 604 while it has stood as 12, 05,254 at the ending of year-2016. Therefore, new pending suits stand 7, 48,650 in this period. On the contrary, at the end of year-2016 the total pending cases in session courts and judicial magistrate courts stand as 1512958 whereas at the end of 2007 there were total 872503 cases as pending (The Supreme Court of Bangladesh, 2008 & 2016). Therefore, new backlogs are 6,40,455. Another important thing is that in civil courts, sessions and criminal courts in all cases the disposal rate of cases or suits are lesser than to filing new cases except last two years disposal rate of cases in the judicial magistrate courts. The study has identified some problems which are directly responsible for backlogs in civil and criminal justice: shortage of judicial officers, inadequate manpower or having no stenographers for assistant or senior assistant judges courts, lengthy trial system, analogue system, backdated procedural laws, fake cases, absence of separate investigation cell, lack of adequate accommodation for discharging judicial functions and dual rule are mainly and directly responsible behind backlogs of cases in our judiciary. Without removing and resolving such problems, civil and criminal justice are not possible to be ensured properly and due time or even reasonable time. Along with removing and resolving the identified problems, the following steps can be considered for ensuring quick civil and criminal justice.

-Introducing separate establishment to the post of session judge

-Implementing the proposal of Law Commission-Bangladesh regarding appointment of judges in proportion to the people of the country in comparing with neighboring country;

-Establishing separate and distinct ADR courts where a civil suit is to be filed first for ADR resolution; in case of failure of ADR Resolution the suit can be filed in the ordinary civil courts;

ADR system should be introduced in criminal proceeding for compoundable offences

-Utilizing mobile SMS facilities in case of summons;

-Introducing incentive for disposal of more civil suits;

-Introducing rigorous punishment for false cases and setting minimum five lakh as compensatory cost for fake suits.

References:

Abdul Wadud v Nazmul Hossain [2009] 14 BLC 14

Aminullah v Bangladesh [2008] 13 BLC 224

Alam, M Shah, 2000. *A Possible Way out of Backlog in Our Judiciary*. Dhaka: The Daily Star, 16th April, 2000. Available at: http://ruchichowdhury.tripod.com/a_possible_way_out_of_backlog_in_our_judiciary.htm

Ahmed, Tofail (2011). *Britto O Brithantho: Bikendrikaran, Shathania Shasan, Rajnithi O Unnayan Bhabna* (in Bangla). Dhaka: Agamee Prokashani.

Annual Reports, 2008-2016, HCD, Supreme Court of Bangladesh

Anwar Hossain Chowdhury v Bangladesh 1989 BLD (Spl) 1(8th Amendment Case)

Asaduzzaman v Bangladesh, 2009 BLD 643

Austin, Caroline, 2017. *Research Question*. [viewed 5th June, 2018]. Available at: https://www.quora.com/What-is-the-difference-between-a-research-question-and-a-resea...

Ain-o-Salish Kendra v Bangladesh (2011) 63 DLR 95

AKM Shafiuddin v Bangladesh (2012) 64 DLR 508

Anon, 1978.The Speedy Trial Act and Separation of Powers: United States v. Howard. Harvard Law Review, 91(8), 1925-1933 [viewed 6th March, 2018]. Available From: http:// www.jstor.org/stable/1340415

Anon (2016). 'End 'dual rule' in judiciary'. *The Daily Star*, 1st Nov.2016. p.1, [accessed at 6.6.2018]. https://www.thedailystar.net/frontpage/end-dual-rule-judiciary-1307422

Bangladesh & ors v. BLAST & ors 8 SCOB [2016] AD1

Bangladesh Sangbadpatra Parishad v Bangladesh [1991] 43 DLR (AD) 126

Bangladesh Jatiyo Mahila Ainjibi Samity (BJMAS) v Ministry of Home Affairs and Others, 2008 BLD, 580

Bangladesh v Md. Aftabuddin, 2010 BLD (AD) 1

Bangladesh v Ministry of Home Affairs [2008]16 BLT 264

Bangladesh & ors v BLAST & ors [2016] 8 SCOB AD 1

Biswas, Dr. Zahidul Islam (2012, September). 'Do We Have an Independent Judiciary?' 6 (9) *Forum the Daily Star*. Retrieved from https://works.be pres s.com/zahid/8/download/

BLAST & Others v Bangladesh & Others 1SCOB (2015) AD 2

BLAST v. Bangladesh 55 DLR 363

BLAST v. Bangladesh (2011) 63 DLR 1

BLAST v Bangladesh (2011) 63 DLR 643

Camion, Clement, 2016. Three Trade-offs to Efficient Dispute Resolution. In: Benyekhelf et al. *eAccess to Justice*. Ottawa: University of Ottawa Press, [viewed 6th March, 2018]. Available From: http:// www.jstor.org/stable /j.ctt1wn0qx3.18

Chairman RAJUK v. Abdur Rouf Chowdhury (2009) 61 DLR (AD)28

Chief Justice Speech at National Judicial Conference, 2016 held at Dhaka 24-25, Dec. 2016. Available at www. Supremecourt.gov.bd. Accessed on 7.9.17

Concord Pragatee Consortium Ltd v. *BPDB* (2014) 66 DLR 475

Dewanbagh Darbar Sharif v Bangladesh [2002]54 DLR 413

Dr. M. O Ghani v Dr. A.N.M. Mahmud [1996] 18 DLR (SC) 517

Dr. Mohiuddin Farooque v. Bangladesh (2003) 55DLR 69

Dr. Mohuuddin Farooque v. Bangladesh (1997) 48 DLR 438

Dr. Mohuuddin Farooque v Bangladesh [1997] 49 DLR (AD)1

Dr. Shipra v Bangladesh (2009)14 BLC 561

'Draft of dowry act incorporates punishment for false case'. The Financial Express, 7th May, 2018. [accessed at 6.6.2018]. https://thefinancialexpress.com.bd/national/draft-of-dowry-act-incorporates-punishment-for-false-case-1525693846

Draft Universal Declaration on the Independence of Justice, 1989. Available at: https://www.cristidanilet.ro/docs/Shingvi%20Declaration.pdf (Last visited September 11, 2018).

Edruk Ltd v Bangladesh [2009] 14 BLC 102

Emran Ahmed v. *Bangladesh* (2012) 64 DLR 462

Emdadul Haque v DG, Education 60 DLR (2008)

Hasnat, Mahadi Al (2017). Injustices drove Hazrat, daughter to suicide. *Dhaka Tribune*, 6th May. [accessed at 6.6.2018]. https://www.dhakatribune.com/bangladesh/2017/05/06/injustices-drove-hazrat-daughter-suicide

Hasuba Begum v Ministry of Home Affairs, 2010 BLD 481

Halim ,Abdul and Siddiki, N.E. (2010). *The Legal System of Bangladesh (*2nd edn, University Publication, Dhaka)

Haque,Justice Mohammad Hamidul. (2010) *Trial of Civil Suits and Criminal Cases,* (Author himself, 1st edn,)

Hoque, Kazi Ebadul, *Administration of Justice in Bangladesh,* 1st Edition, Asiatic Society of Bangladesh, Dhaka, 2003, p.53.

Hossain, Md. Milan (2017)., "Effective Judiciary and Citizens' Rights- A study: Bangladesh Perspective" 3(1), *AJLEG* (2017) available at: www.ajleg.net.au/index.php/AJLEG/article/view/28 (Last visited on August 28, 2018).

HRPB v. *Bangladesh* (2011) 63 DLR 71

Huda, MN. 'Independent Judiciary a must for democracy', The Daily Star (Dhaka, 27March2017), available at: https://www.thedailystar.net/opinion/straight-line/independent-judiciary-must-democracy-1381690. (last visited on on 12 January 2020).

Human Rights for Peace for Bangladesh v Bangladesh, 2010 BLD 125

Idrisur Rahman v. *Bangladesh* (2009) 61 DLR 523

International Covenant on Civil and Political Rights, 1966

Islam, Mahmudul (2012). *Constitutional Law of Bangladesh*. 3rd ed. Dhaka: Mullick Brother

Islam, M Rafiqul. "Independence of Judiciary-The Masdar Case." *The Daily Star* (Dhaka, 10 March 2014). available at: https://www.thedaily star.net/independence-of-the-judiciary-the-masdar-case-14760 (Last visit on September 8, 2018).

Khan, Mizanur Rahman (2016, January 27). 'An Interview with Mr. Anisul Haque, Honable Minister, Law & Justice, Govt. of Republic of Bangladesh' *The Daily Prothom Alo* p. 1.

Khan, Sharier (2015). Denying just won't do. The Daily Star, Dhaka, 2nd November, p.1

Korban v Bangladesh [2003]55 DLR 194

Law Commission-Bangladesh, 2015. An Additional Report for Reducing Backlogs in Courts and Few Recommendations [viewed 6th March, 2018]. Available From: http:// www.lc.gov.bd/reports.htm

Liton, Shakhawat and Sarkar, Ahuthosh (2015, August 6). 'Mobile Court Trials "often violate rights"' *The Daily Star* p.1.

Locke, John, *Two Treaties of Government* 168 (New edn, Vol. 5, 1823, Para 144 available at: https://www.yorku.ca/comninel/courses/3025pdf/Locke.pdf (Last visited on May 31, 2018).

Malik, Shadin (2016, June 29). 'Hatee Gora Gelo Tol' (Horse Elephant Gone to Under). *The Prothom Alo*, p. 11.

Maulana Syed Rezaul Haque Chadpuri v Bangladesh Jamaat-e-Islam (Spl Original) 66 DLR (2014) 14

Md. Abdul Bari v Bangladesh 2010 BLD 465

Mohammad Ali v BD [1995] 47 DLR 350

Metro Makers & Developers Ltd v. Bangladesh Environmental Lawyers' Association Ltd (BELA) and others (2013) 65 DLR (AD) 181

MFB, Hussain (2015). 'An Appraisal of Criminal Investigation in Bangladesh'. 60(2) Journal of Asiatic Society (Humanities). Available at: www.asiaticsociety.org.bd/journal/H_December_2015/1%20H_885_D2015.pdf (Last visited on September 15, 2018).

Mobile Court Case 2017 (writ no. 8437 & 10482 of 2011, and 4879 of 2012) Retrieved from www.supremecourt.gov.bd/resources/documents/382548_WP8437of2011.pdf

Momin Motors Co. v RTA Dacca [1962]14 DLR (SC) 102

Montesqueiu. *The Spirit of the Laws* 157 (Cambridge University Press, Cambridge, 1989), cited also in Sarkar Ali Akkas, Independence and Accountability of Judiciary-A Critical Review 17 (Center for Rights and Governance, Dhaka-1000, 2004).

Monzil Morshed v Bangladesh [2008]16 BLT 327

Motala, Ziyad, 2001. Judicial Accountability and court performance standards: managing court delay. *The Comparative and International Law Journal of Southern Africa,* 34(2), 172-187[viewed 6th March, 2018]. Available From: http:// www.jstor.org/stable/23251123

Mrs. Parvin Akter v Rajuk, [1998]18 BLD 117, para 15

Nasiruddin v *Secretary, LGRD* [1999]51 DLR (AD) 213

Nazrul Islam v Bangladesh [2006] 58 DLR 431

Paley, W (1824). "Moral and Political Philosophy" 345 (1824) cited in SAM J Ervin, 'Separation of Power: Judicial Independence' (1970) 35 Law and Contemporary Problems 108-127, available at: https://scholarship.law.duke.edu/cgi/viewcontent.cgi?referer=https://www.google.com/&httpsredir=1&article=3279&context=lcp (Last visited on May 27, 2018).

Press Information Bureau, Govt. of India, Separate Investigation and Prosecution Cadre Proposed for Speedy Criminal Justice, 2012, available at: http://pib.nic.in/newsite/PrintRelease.aspx?relid=80575(Last visited on September 15, 2018).

Professor *Muhammad Yunus* v. *Bangladesh* (2012) 64 DLR (AD)152

Professor Nurul Islam v. Bangladesh, (2000) 52 DLR 413

Rajab Ali v East Pakistan [1958] 10 DLR 385

Secretary, Ministry of Finance v. Masdar Hossain and others, 52 DLR (AD) 82, Para. 89.

Sinha, Surendra Kumar, 2016. Address in Inaugural Session, National Judicial Conference , 24-25th December, 2016, Dhaka Bangladesh [viewed 11.5.17]. Available from:http://www.supremecourt.gov.bd/resources/contents/CJ_Speech_National_Judicial_Conferrence_2016-Inaugural_Session.pdf

Sinha, Surendra Kumar, 2016. The Contribution of the Judiciary. The Ittefaq, Dhaka, 25th December, 2016, p. 8, Available from: http://epaper.ittefaq.com.bd/?archiev=yes&arch_date=25-12-2016#

Shamim, Eqramul Haque (2019, June 20). Backlog in the Judiciary V Disposal. *LawyersClub Bangladesh.com.* (2019, June 20). Retrieved from http://lawyersclubbangladesh.com/2019/06/20/

Shahidul Islam v Bangladesh [2008] 60 DLR 710

Staff Correspondent, (2016, April 3). 'Fair Justice Not Possible for Murder of Tanu under old laws'. *The Prothom Alo,* p. 1.

State v Anjali Devi (2009) 61 DLR 738

Takwani, C.K, *Lectures On Administrative Law,* 5th Edition, Eastern Book Company, Lucknow, 2012, p. 243.

The High Court Division, Supreme Court of Bangladesh (2008-2016) Static on the Cases of Bangladesh, Annual Reports 2008-2016.

Thean, LP, 2003. *Judicial Independence and Effectiveness* [online] [*viewed* 10 January 2015]. Available from: http:// www. Aseanlawassociation.org/docs/w1_sing.pdf

Tipu, MSI and Shaon, AI. "Why we need an independent public prosecution service" *DhakaTribune,* available at: https://www.dhakatribune.com/bangladesh/2017/07/06/need-independent-public-prosecution-service (Last visited on 10 January 2020).

The World Bank. 'Legal and Judicial Capacity Building Project, Finance and Private Sector Department: South Asia Region.' available at: http://documents.worldbank.org/curated/en/223531468007223731/pdf/ICR120001Public0Disclosed0July0121.pdf (Last visit on September 8, 2018).

UN Basic Principles on the Independence of the Judiciary, 1985, available at: https://www.un.org/ruleoflaw/blog/document/basic-principles-on-the-independence-of-the-judiciary/ (Last visited on September 11, 2018).

The Constitution of the People's Republic of Bangladesh

The Civil Court Act 1887

The Code of Civil Procedure, 1908, Sec. 9

The Code of Criminal Procedure, 1898

The Evidence Act, 1872, ss.137-138

The Penal Code, 1860

Universal Declaration of Human Rights, 1948

Z. I. Khan Panna v Bangladesh & ors 7 SCOB (2016) HCD 7

16th Amendment case (Civil Appeal No.06 of 2017). Retrieved from http://www.supremecourt.gov.bd/resources/documents/1082040_C.A.6of17.pdf

www.ingramcontent.com/pod-product-compliance
Lightning Source LLC
LaVergne TN
LVHW022052200926
848481LV00003B/886
* 9 7 9 8 8 9 2 4 8 7 6 4 1 *